Anton Friedrich Justus Thibaut, William Henry Gladstone

On Purity in Musical Art

Anton Friedrich Justus Thibaut, William Henry Gladstone

On Purity in Musical Art

ISBN/EAN: 9783337084820

Printed in Europe, USA, Canada, Australia, Japan

Cover: Foto ©Thomas Meinert / pixelio.de

More available books at **www.hansebooks.com**

ON
Purity in Musical Art

BY

ANTON FRIEDRICH JUSTUS THIBAUT

HEIDELBERG, 1825.

TRANSLATED FROM THE GERMAN

BY

W. H. GLADSTONE

A fine book on Music is that 'On Purity in Musical Art,' by Thibaut. Read it often as you grow older.—R. SCHUMANN.

LONDON
JOHN MURRAY, ALBEMARLE STREET
1877

[All rights reserved.]

PURITY IN MUSICAL ART

DEDICATED

BY THE TRANSLATOR

TO

The Bach Choir,

AND, IN PARTICULAR, TO ITS CONDUCTOR,

OTTO GOLDSCHMIDT.

CONTENTS.

		PAGE
I.	On the Chorale	1
II.	On Church Music other than the Chorale .	36
III.	On Popular Melodies	66
IV.	On the Instruction to be derived from Good Models	83
V.	On Effect	94
VI.	On the Use of Instruments . . .	106
VII.	On a Careful Judging of Great Masters' Works	127
VIII.	On a Liberal Judgment . . .	149
IX.	On Misadaptations of Text . . .	157
X.	On Choral Societies	168

PREFACE.

THE fact that this Essay was first published more than half a century ago, might seem, at first sight, to render its translation now a work of doubtful utility. But, inasmuch as it is still in demand in Germany, as is proved by the publication of the Fifth Edition as recently as in 1875, and looking to the great extension of the study and practice of music in our own country, I am persuaded that it will be read both with interest and with profit in England.

Anton Friedrich Justus Thibaut was first Professor of Jurisprudence at Heidelberg, and author of several important treatises on Roman and modern law, published between 1797 and 1818. The present Essay appeared

Preface. in 1825, when the author was fifty-one years of age. His friend, Dr. Bähr, who, after his death in 1840, edited the fourth edition, describes the book, on its first appearance, as a voice crying in the wilderness, and summoning men to a musical repentance. It denounced in no measured terms the musical vices of the day, and held up as a pattern the great works of the early composers, which posterity was not ashamed to ignore, and even to despise. It condemned the folly of sacrificing time and talent in ephemeral compositions, when so many immortal works only needed to be brought to light and made known to be appreciated, and pointed in particular to the Palestrina age, as the golden period of Church music, and a mine of inexhaustible wealth. At no other period, Thibaut held, has so high an idea of the real nature of Church music prevailed, or so masterly a conformity to its true end been displayed.

Between Church and Oratorio music he draws an important distinction, too often forgotten in our day. In the former, the one prevailing idea is the personal relation of the individual to his Maker; in the latter, we contemplate, as it were at some distance, the most striking pictures of Sacred History. And, in these two great departments, he claims the foremost place as for Palestrina in the one, so for Handel in the other.

Thibaut's undisguised admiration for the old masters exposed him to a charge of undue partiality, from which his editor defends him. "I never saw," he says, "any lover of music who was so exactly the reverse of one-sided, and who was less prejudiced in favour of particular authors and compositions. Antiquity was not with him the test of excellence, but he rejoiced in excellence wherever he found it, and never asked from what author or from what period it came. Nor, again, was he blind to the weak points of those very composers whom he accounted the greatest. The treasures which, with an exceedingly fine instinct, he restored to the light of day, are such as will never grow old, but rather will bloom and thrive when the more favourite productions of to-day shall have long withered and decayed."

The last sentence refers to the large and valuable collection of vocal music made by Thibaut, and used by the small but famous choir that held its practice-meetings in his house and under his superintendence at Heidelberg. It comprised works of the principal Italian, Flemish, French, and German composers, representing some forty of the fifteenth and sixteenth centuries, and some seventy of the seventeenth and eighteenth; besides a large collection of ancient chorales and of national melodies of all countries. It may now be consulted in the Royal

Library at Munich. Thus it will be seen that Thibaut speaks to us not merely as a cultivated musical student and amateur, but with the authority attaching to personal experience in the conduct of a choral society. Dr. Bähr, himself an active member of it, speaks of the enthusiasm and the judgment of his leader as revealing to him a new world in music such as he had never previously imagined—a source of best and purest pleasure.

In choosing for his Essay the title of "Purity in Musical Art," Thibaut had in view not so much technical as moral purity. Music he considered not a mere study, nor a mere amusement, but rather as a moral agency. Pure music springs from a natural and healthy impulse, and, in its turn, reacts to the edifying and refining of the mind; while music of a different origin operates, like bad literature, to enervate and demoralise.

Hence he fiercely assails all musical shallowness and frivolity, and, Dr. Bähr tells us, would only admit into his choir those of whose sympathy for what was high and pure he felt assured.

The lofty conception of music, and, in particular, of Church music, unfolded in the following pages, is one that we may well study and imbibe, for it will hardly be denied that in England, music, in spite of the great and growing interest taken in it, has certain unwholesome tendencies, requiring an enlightened judgment for their correction. To speak only of our Church music, we find the lines of demarcation, here so strongly insisted upon by Thibaut, between the Church and the World, blurred and even obliterated in all the branches of our musical Worship. Technical skill and ability we have in abundance, but the instinct to reject what is unfitted, and to construct what is conducive, to the highest purposes of religion is no less rare.

While the noble traditions of our own Cathedral school still, to some extent, survive, the music of the Palestrina age—the firstfruits of genius and enthusiasm in the cause of the Church—is, practically, a sealed book to us. Congregational singing, with its heart-stirring power, is seldom to be heard. Words, which should stand in the most intimate relation to music, are often degraded into its mere appendages. A fond idea of progress seems ever to entice us away from what we have, to something else that we know not of. These are tendencies against which this little volume is a protest. Not a few, I hope, will recognise the general truth and justice of that protest—will inhale the pure and healthy air that breathes in its pages, and catch something of the enthusiasm that dictated them.

Were testimony wanting to the opportuneness of Thibaut's plea on behalf of the older music, it might be found in the remarkable activity and enterprise which have been shown, particularly in Germany, since he wrote, in the direction indicated by him. Its nature and extent may be at once collected by glancing at Eitner's Index (Berlin, 1871). The list of compilations there given is far too long to detail; but I may mention the publications of the Musical Antiquarian Society in our own country; the collection of the Prince de la Moskowa in France; that of D. Hilarion Eslava in Spain; the Anthologia Classica de Milano, and Alfieri's fine edition of "Palestrina" in Italy; whilst in Germany we have Proske and Schrems' "Musica Divina," Von Witt's "Palestrina," the collections of Rochlitz, Commer, and Bock; and last, not least, the annual issues of the Bach and Handel Societies.

The way, then, is open, if only the will be forthcoming, to the fulfilment of Thibaut's exhortation to cultivate the great works of all times and all nations. Such a task has been from time to time essayed. It was essayed by the Ancient Concerts of the last generation; and, considering the limited material then at command, with great success. It is now essayed with ampler resources and with every good promise, by the Amateur Society to whom this Translation is dedicated. To all those who, in a right spirit, combine for such a purpose our Author promises a rich reward. May the members of the Bach Choir find in their labour of love that bright sun and that life-long pleasure of which Thibaut speaks as the result of his own experience! And may their example revive and encourage the practice of Choral Music, for its own sake, in its best and noblest forms!

W. H. G.

ON THE CHORALE.

On the Chorale.

It has perhaps never been so generally acknowledged as at the present time that the groundwork of all true knowledge must necessarily lie in the historical study and acquisition of standard works that have come down to us. It is only by thus profiting by the lessons of others that fresh energy can safely be applied towards the advancement of truth. Acquaintance with the older masterpieces may also have the great negative advantage of convincing worthless pretensions of their futility, and of diverting them from the business of production to the quiet enjoyment and diffusion of the model works we have inherited from past ages. Men of real genius, like Plato, Raphael, and Shakespeare, are phenomena of ex-

History the groundwork of knowledge.

On the Chorale.

tremely rare occurrence; but it has been theirs to sway generation after generation, and to exert a beneficial influence for thousands of years. Hence it is of all conceits the most pitiable for any one to dispense with the study of the classics from confidence in his own powers, and so, in effect, declare that he considers himself on a par with the great spirits of bygone time. All our young men of education make it almost a point of honour to revert to the model authors of antiquity; and any one who was setting up for a painter would assuredly no more venture to pronounce the study of the works of Raphael, Michael Angelo, Van Eyck, and Dürer, to be superfluous, than would a youthful poet venture to come out with a new Iliad, or a new King Lear, without acquainting himself with the immortal works of Homer or Shakespeare. Hence in poetry, painting, and architecture, we now have a freshness and life which cannot but please, though it happens often enough that a want of genius and power causes the best intentions to fall short of the complete fulfilment of their aim.

On the Chorale.

It is in music alone that an arrogance, that disdains all history, is the order of the day, although the greatest masters of the period preceding our own showed us a better example. There was nothing on which Handel, Hasse, and Graun were more eagerly bent than on the thorough prosecution of musical study in Italy. They did not indeed follow the example of most of our professors, who take every opportunity of showing off with a few bravura pieces laboriously mastered, and think that classical taste is to be found among the audiences of the concert-room; but, whilst composing fine works, and offering them to the judgment of the public, they took care to study the standard works of others for themselves, and cultivated an intimate acquaintance with the most eminent masters. Sebastian Bach, again, who was prevented from travel-

Neglect of this principle in music at the present day, and disregard of the example of the most distinguished musicians.

On the Chorale. ling, studied intently the works of other masters—Caldara, the immortal Venetian, being one of his especial favourites. Even Mozart, though his genius rendered him well nigh independent of others, yet held the chief works of his predecessors—those of Handel and Sebastian Bach in particular—in high esteem; and it is owing, primarily, to his edition of the "Messiah" that Handel's reputation has outlived an age of musical shallowness. But now, how utterly changed is all this! We see now an almost absolute reliance on individual powers, an unlimited amount of original composition, and, for the most part, a contemptuous disregard for what is called antiquated. Authors, to whom Handel and Hasse could bow the knee, such as Antonio Lotti and Alessandro Scarlatti, are nowadays not known even by name to most people; and even our own incomparable Handel is, excepting in a few places, not generally treated with that respect which is due to his inexhaustible, and in many ways unique genius. And this ignorance of and indifference to history applies not merely to what we call the Church and Oratorio styles. Even with opera, historical knowledge does not, in general, reach back beyond Gluck. Handel's operas have fallen into disuse, and if any one were to refer to those of Caldara and Lotti, he would almost be laughed at. It is just the same with the fugue. Things, indeed, so named are strung together, after a fashion, by thousands yearly, conformable to rule, but destitute of life; but the kind of fugue that Scarlatti wrote in the works which Hasse and Handel admired, is known to hardly one in a thousand of our self-complacent young composers, organists, and teachers. In the same way we are daily overwhelmed with a deluge of songs; but the study of ancient national airs, which often have an indescribable charm, and afford a profound insight into the character of different peoples, is altogether out of date; though here, were it only from the vigour and vitality of the

On the Chorale.

ancient communities, something remarkable could not but have been looked for.

The causes of this sad state of things are, indeed, sufficiently obvious. To comprehend a Madonna of Raphael, to be impressed by a cathedral like Cologne, to take in the great things of Shakespeare, nothing more is requisite than a healthy perception and taste, and a more or less educated intelligence; and in architecture, painting, and poetry, it is impossible to disguise failures. But the masterpieces of music are as gold buried deep in the earth, which few have the ability and the will to bring to light. A number of the finest things consist of MS. scores scattered about here and there. Even a journey to Italy is not of much avail without skilled investigation, for even there the choicest works (excepting several which are performed in the Sistine Chapel) are as good as dead and buried. One may travel from Milan to Naples without hearing a syllable about Vittoria or Lotti. Now, who has the means of

On the Chorale.

Musical treasures difficult of acquisition.

obtaining these full scores? and how many, I ask in all seriousness, of our ordinary musicians can read with facility scores that are neither slight in texture, nor written in the modern notation? But, after the material is found, and the notation understood, we are still at the beginning of our task. The picture must, as it were, be painted afresh, so as to assume its due complexion; a competent staff must execute the piece with a skill and enthusiasm corresponding to that which produced it; and where are the men who can don the armour of the giants of old? Hence, our crack players, music-directors, and teachers, are shy of the old music, and try in every way to throw ridicule on the countless musical treasures we have to boast of; and in this they succeed with the utmost ease. For the public, whether of low or high degree, have no musical principles of their own; they must just take what they find offered; and under these circumstances, the professors have no difficulty in acquiring a

On the Chorale.

Old music shunned by the profession,

who guide the public.

On the Chorale.

Vicious elements in music easily masked.

decisive influence by their mechanical skill. Moreover, there is this danger with music. If, in a picture, we find a limb out of drawing, or anything immoral, a healthy eye at once sees sufficient reason for censure, and turns away for very shame, at least in the presence of others. But in music there may be concealed all manner of impure, morbid, and immoral elements; and thus the rubbish that, if presented by the pen or pencil, could not, for credit's sake, fail to be rejected, comes to be swallowed wholesale by the unwary. Hence the composers and professors of our day have an easy game to play. To stoop to the sensational, the uncouth, the absurd, and the meretricious, touches only too many responsive chords; and a connoisseur, when he hears the exclamation, "Oh, how beautiful!" often has to hold his tongue for politeness' sake, because the true comment on such a phrase could not be made aloud without affront. When once the public have their ears attuned to a vulgar and depraved style of music, their taste becomes fixed, and they, in their turn, become despots over the professors; just as in a case of indigestion and headache, the one aggravates the other, till nothing remains but to wish for a happy despatch. Plato, in his day, inveighed against demoralising music. What would he say if he had to listen to the gymnastics of our day, which only require a few extra fingers to extinguish all we call art?—compositions in such complete contradiction to nature, ranging between the extremes of feebleness and license, steeped in passion, and yet rarely rising to the height of real inspiration! We stand, in fact, in regard to music, as we have it in everyday life (for here, as elsewhere, I make no reference to the exceptions which, happily, there are), in scarcely so good a position as we should in regard to the drama, were the latter not still in some degree influenced by a better spirit, and were we reduced to whatever the fancy of our ordinary actors was pleased to set before us.

On the Chorale.

Consequent depravity of modern taste.

On the Chorale.

Abuse of music in the Church intolerable.

Would that this could all be passed over in silence, as applying only to concert-rooms and theatres! If it be too outrageous for us there, we can stay away, and try to console ourselves with something better. But the church must not and ought not to be burdened with the vices of music. For her members are bound to her by a moral tie; and if, instead of religious fervour being stimulated to the highest pitch, the perversion of the noble and beautiful causes them nothing but scandal, not a word can be said for such an abuse. Yet this is, alas! everywhere the case, though nowhere should it be easier to preserve the best of the old music from oblivion than in our very churches. For if we paid no heed to the silly fancies of fashion, we could safely reckon on the people, of their own accord, always treating the works of antiquity, as such, with the deepest respect, because they perceive clearly that this is almost the sole means by which health and purity of manners can be preserved.

But, even apart from this, there were the strongest reasons for preserving the original chorales of each communion pure and unimpaired. For, whatever art may do by way of addition or embellishment, it will always remain an indisputable fact that melodies which are, as it were, the natural and transparent outflow of an impassioned, deeply-stirred spirit, possess an indefinable charm that never grows old, and, as is the case with many national airs, live on ever fresh and blooming in a nation's memory, if they be not destroyed by external influences. Now, all our communions had, in the early days of their existence, a period of intense enthusiasm, which will never return; and, during that period of burning zeal for religion, each one did its utmost to improve its choral music, under the guidance of men thoroughly conversant with the true church modes. How can we then explain the arrogance of the present age, so cold, so feeble, and so utterly worldly in religious matters, in dis-

On the Chorale.

Folly of neglecting the ancient melodies.

On the Chorale.

playing, even in the church, nothing but its own productions, and heedlessly discarding all that would fill true Christians with joy and delight? Yet this is what has happened in the greatest degree where one would have least expected it, and in the smallest degree where one would have most expected it.

The Russian Church alone has adhered to the ancient tunes.

It is of the Russo-Greek Church that this last must be predicated. She alone has adhered to the past, so far as was possible in a changeful world, with an almost iron tenacity, and has retained much that may carry us back perhaps to the second or third century. The grandeur of her ancient tunes is ever the wonder of competent judges; and it was a current anecdote in St. Petersburg, not long ago, that a well-known Parisian composer, after hearing some of them in the Imperial Chapel, bitterly exclaimed on coming out, "Is it to St. Petersburg that I must come to hear for the first time real church-music?" It is, indeed, supposed that, since the twelfth century, and especially since the reign of Catherine II., much that is new has crept in; but as regards the liturgy and the part to be taken by the congregation, the music remains in all essential features unchanged. This makes it all the more to be regretted that no one has attempted to make it known in its entirety to the public, because the study of it would, without a doubt, as I am convinced from experience, throw much light upon the Greek modes.

On the Chorale.

The Roman Church had of all others, in virtue of its constitution, the most cogent reasons for retaining the great primitive tunes known as Ambrosian or Gregorian; those (so far as my knowledge of them goes) truly heavenly and sublime songs and intonations, which, conceived by genius and adorned by art in the early and best times of the Church, lay hold of the soul more powerfully than many of our modern compositions directly aimed at effect. Yet the Sistine Chapel, though remarkably constant to the works of the intermediate period, scarcely seems to

The music of the Sistine Chapel is of a later date.

On the Chorale.

view these primitive strains with equal favour. Be that as it may, it is certain that any one who wished to be thoroughly informed on the subject of the Ambrosian and Gregorian melodies, would be unable to obtain satisfaction anywhere in Italy. In Germany he would, at best, get a quotation or two from Forkel's compilation; as for anything further, it would seem almost a point of honour to profess entire ignorance. How indeed could it be otherwise, when those who sit in high places positively repudiate these tunes? How appropriate would it have been that the Cathedral of Cologne should be the temple wherein the sublime bequests of the great olden time should find their sanctuary! Yet what has happened? In 1741 there appeared in Cologne, formally sanctioned by the Elector, and highly praised by the Censors, the chorale book, which has since come so extensively into use, entitled "The new Church and Household Hymn-book, sacred to God and the Lamb, for the Daughter of Sion pursuing

The Ambrosian and Gregorian melodies ignored in Germany.

Inferior hymn-books issued by authority.

the Triune path of perfection to the heavenly Jerusalem;"* and this very hymn-book is so full of dance-like sing-song melodies as would be absolutely incredible, did it not appear from the preface that, to obtain sufficient variety, the editor had been careful to engage a number of different hands in its preparation; "as most of the tunes of the old common hymn-book have become corrupt, or because so few of them are of an edifying character." It may, without exaggeration, be said that the semi-sacred, semi-romantic manual of devotion and entertainment, called "The Mock Nightingale," and published, with music by a Jesuit, at Cologne in 1649, is, with all its romance, more spiritual in character than this only too famous hymn-book.

On the Chorale.

Proceeding now to the Hussites' hymns, the only thing about them we find to console

Admirable character of the Hussite Chorales.

* "Neues Gott und den Lamm geheiligtes Kirchen- und Haus-Gesang der auf dem dreifachen Wege der Vol- kommenheit nach dem himmlischen Jerusalem wandern- den Tochter Sion."

On the Chorale.

us is that they were highly esteemed and used by Luther, and that they are still to some extent retained, modernised no doubt in many respects, in Moravian churches. Yet these tunes are of all others those which least deserved to be forgotten. For, emanating from a stock which has to this day distinguished itself far and wide for eminent musical capacity—the outpourings of intense fervency of spirit under circumstances of oppression and persecution—these Hussite Chorales bear the stamp of a spiritual power, an humble resignation, and a moral dignity, that can scarcely be matched elsewhere. Yet Lutherans have clean forgotten them; and all the more unpardonably so, because this Hussite hymnbook is said to have been considered so dangerous by the Jesuits, that, with the exception of a few copies, one of which has by good luck fallen into my hands, they bought it up and burnt it. This would have been an admirable reason for patronising the proscribed work by issuing a large new edition.

Strangely neglected by Lutherans.

But, until quite recently, no one thought of such a thing; while the most worthless compositions were all the time being published, as though they were treasures necessary for the public to possess.

On the Chorale.

What Luther did for the Chorale—how he, as it were, blazed and consumed away in his passion for sacred music, singing with his choir-boys right into the night—how, according to Walter, an eyewitness, it was impossible for him to flag or tire of singing, and how his soul seemed ever more and more aglow with it—all this is notorious. Moreover, many excellent observations of his on music are in every one's mouth. Yet the singing in the churches which he founded speedily degenerated. As early as 1628 appeared the Chorale book of that eminent man Henry Schütz, which was in many respects adapted to the newly prevalent taste. The preface modestly declares that it was necessary to make concessions to the spirit of the time; but the compiler adds, with a sort of

Luther's passion for singing.

Subsequent deterioration of the Chorale.

On the Chorale.

compunction, "I must, however, confess that I consider some of the old melodies to have been the creation of celestial seraphims rather than of men." Every one who knows anything of music knows how these strains have in later days been translated into modern scales, and overladen with abrupt transitions and modulations. Sebastian Bach, indeed, before whose grandeur we are all ready to bow when he exhibits himself to us in perfect simplicity, might have proved a veritable saviour. But his bent lay more towards perfecting his art in the direction of florid part-writing, and of rising to its loftiest flights (as indeed other considerable masters have done since) without regard to popular requirements. Hence his four-part chorales, incomparable, no doubt, in themselves, must be accounted unprofitable as regards the people at large, and most of our organists. In fact, so long as people were content to be entirely ignorant of the genuine old church-tones, any adequate remedy was out of the question; for the merely

Bach's treatment of the Chorale not designed for popular use.

Acquiescence in ignorance made reform impossible.

theoretical works on the subject then in vogue threw no light upon them. It may be said, indeed, that a general search should have been made for ancient authorities which might convey to intelligent minds the requisite information. But laborious undertakings like this were by no means agreeable suggestions. And yet what a mine there was to explore! Palestrina, the most famous master of the Church school, following trustworthy traditions, set the Magnificat, with infinite ingenuity, eight times over to the eight Church tones, for four voices. Any one might have possessed himself of this work, but it has been suffered to lie buried in oblivion; and Busby, in his "History of Music," has lately rolled another large stone over its grave, by informing us that "Palestrina composed a Magnificat for eight voices."

If, again, we take the tunes of the Calvinists, we shall find that they too have their share of innovations. Calvin caused the Psalms to be put into French verse, and the

On the Chorale.

Though the means were at hand.

Similar corruption of the Calvinistic tunes.

On the Chorale.

melodies to them to be then arranged, in complete accordance with the original Church tones, by Bourgeois, and that great master Goudimel, who afterwards fell a victim to religious fanaticism in the Massacre of St. Bartholomew. The text of this splendidly executed work was subsequently translated into German by Ambrose Lobwasser, who immediately revised the music, introduced secular modes, and changed the plain song into four-part harmony, while often giving the leading part to the tenor. This secular tendency is visible in the very first edition (Herborn, 1666), and still more so in the second (Frankfort, 1711), the preface to which says, significantly enough, "We have omitted what seemed to be devoid of any particular edification, and changed each Psalm to its natural and proper tune." Degglar, in his edition (Schaffhausen, 1761), left the text as it stood. Nevertheless, the excellence of the work is visible on every page.

Thus, as time went on, has the genuine

PURITY IN MUSICAL ART.

Chorale been always less and less excusably maltreated and neglected. But there accrued yet another evil. Our old organists knew hardly anything besides sacred music, and the fugues and canons which had been associated with it; but they were, as a rule, well versed in thorough base. If they erred, it was in using ornament for a spiritual, but for no frivolous purpose. But what have we now? Universal neglect of thorough base, and an almost exclusive pursuit of common opera and other inferior music. Anything from this source that gets into the music-master's head in the course of the week, must needs be reproduced in church on Sunday; and in this way we have so often to listen to so much that is secular and inappropriate, that it would be no wonder if some day indignation broke out in the church itself. In Italy also, if we except the Sistine Chapel, the history of which has recently been made known to us in Siever's very interesting notices in the "Allgemeine Musik-

[Side notes: On the Chorale. Add to all this the secular proclivities of modern organists, in Italy as well as Germany.]

On the Chorale.

alische Zeitung," utter lawlessness prevails in this respect. Even in the noble Cathedral of Milan common waltzes and operatic airs are frequently played as preludes to the hymns; and this in the very town where Gregory the Great planted his magnificent schools for singing, and where, 1500 years ago, a whole troop of heathen soldiers, whose duty it was to enter a church in pursuit of Christians, were so deeply moved by the divine hymn that went up from these fervent hearts, that they became converts on the spot.

Reaction in favour of reform.

Meanwhile these gross abuses had, in their turn, a salutary effect in engendering among the congregations an universal desire for the improvement of the Chorale and its accompaniment. Noteworthy writers, too, of the present day have openly declared themselves most strongly in favour of bringing our churches back, in this respect, to their ancient dignity and simplicity: Franz, in his work on the old Church Chorales, 1818;

Mortimer, in his "Choral Song of the time of the Reformation," 1821; and Kocker, both in his remarkable essay on church music, 1823, and also by the part he took, with others, in editing the hymns for four voices in 1825.

On the Chorale.

As it is of the first importance that so grave a matter should be fully elucidated, I take leave to make some further remarks upon it, confining them, however, to the Lutheran Church, to which I belong.

The promoters of a reform of church-music have of late, in several instances, contended for no more than adherence to such melodies as have gained currency in particular localities, as having acquired, once for all, a firm footing, and only requiring to be docked, so to speak, of their wild shoots. But this would seem, in truth, an excess of timidity. If our congregations were capable of substituting inferior modern melodies for fine old ones, they are also capable of retracing their steps, provided organists are instructed where

Such reform should be bold and thorough.

On the Chorale.

No religious prejudice must stand in the way.

to find good music, and how to revive it. The difficulty of doing this is very slight. For the finer old melodies are easily caught, and produce upon educated persons, as I know from many trials, so deep an impression, that all that is necessary is to offer them, and bespeak their acceptance.

But, with the return to ancient music, all sectarian spirit among Protestant communions must disappear, and each must be forward to adopt from another such tunes as are really admirable. What reason can there be that a Lutheran should not sing a fine Calvinistic hymn, or a Calvinist an unexceptionable Lutheran Chorale? Or why should the Hussite Chorales, some of which are quite unapproachable, be abandoned to the Moravians? At this very moment the task of collecting the finer Chorales used in various churches has become a necessity, by reason of a common form of worship having been, in many places, agreed upon by the Lutherans and Calvinists. If, as the result of such wise forbearance, one might contemplate the possibility of a free choice, then even Protestant communions ought to go back to the Ambrosian and Gregorian tunes, and appropriate the best of them. For these tunes sprang from the purest inspiration, and are among the choicest gifts handed down to us by ancient churches; and they ought to be preserved, even by Protestants, as holy relics, because they would form a link with a venerable antiquity, and would thus confer upon Protestant churches an enhanced value in the eyes of the people. Luther himself openly declared for the retention of the fine Catholic tunes, and had several of them printed, remarking that it would be a pity if such precious tunes were suffered to perish. No doubt such an adoption of old Catholic music might be an offence to some of our straitlaced churchwardens. But if we gave in to them, our intercourse with the muses would be limited indeed; and, at this rate, all the old masterpieces of Gothic archi-

On the Chorale.

Adoption of Catholic tunes by Luther.

tecture and painting must fall under the Protestant ban, as being the production of Catholic co-religionists. True Protestants will see more clearly every day that their church would be in the utmost peril if, to favour the views of certain declaimers, all old associations were wiped out; and that people who cannot live without enmity towards those who differ from them in opinion, are simply playing into the hands of Superstition and Mysticism, and by the intolerance which they preach, and by their distrust of all the venerable traditions which we have inherited from the past, are bringing us near to utter disruption.

In the case, however, of the Ambrosian and Gregorian chant, there do seem to be difficulties which hitherto I have not been able to solve, and as to which I would gladly await instruction from persons better informed than myself. And the great question is this—Where are the genuine Ambrosian and Gregorian chants to be found? Our

On the Chorale.

Difficulty of ascertaining the Ambrosian and Gregorian chant.

PURITY IN MUSICAL ART.

musical histories give scanty information on the point, that of Forkel in particular, where bald citations send us, as usual, from pillar to post. There is no doubt that the "Antiphonarium Romanum" contains some of the most ancient hymns and antiphons. But, as it has always been the habit of musicians to pervert and interpolate, that work cannot, unfortunately, be regarded as quite genuine. I have taken all imaginable pains, in Germany, as also in Strasburg, to get a satisfactory account of the Ambrosian and Gregorian chants, but no one could help me. I induced several friends to make inquiries on the subject in Italy, and, in particular, from the master of the papal choir; but their efforts also proved fruitless, though in Rome I was seconded by a German gentleman of high repute, and an influential scholar. This person, however, subsequently made a discovery at St. Gall, likely to prove extremely important. For in the Library there is a MS. of the ninth century, containing the

On the Chorale.

Important MS. at St. Gall.

On the Chorale.

whole Gregorian song, being perhaps the most authentic and genuine document of the kind now in existence. As my professional occupations place it quite beyond my power to devote myself to the deciphering of this MS., I hereby bring it to the notice of musicians, in the hope that some one of them at least will exert himself for the honour of reviving a standard work of bygone time.* Were the only object to gratify ambition, it would be quite within the mark to say that the undertaking of such a task would confer far more renown than any amount of tedious composition, which is, for the most part, about as likely to confer immortality as scribbling on the sand.

Question as to the congregation singing in harmony.

Another important point, now much disputed, relates to the question whether chorales should be arranged in four parts, to be sung by the congregation. The reasons for

---

* A fac-simile of this MS., with an historical notice, is given by Lambillotte.—Antiphonaire de St. Grégoire. Brussels. 1851.

and against have been so often set forth in print, that the controversy may be considered ripe for settlement. And here I have a word to say in retractation of an error. In reviewing Kocker's Essay on Church Music in the "Theological Annals" of December 1824, I took the intention of its esteemed author to be, that the congregation should sing the Chorales in florid four-part harmony. It was against this that my main observations were directed, and I should still adhere to them, were the supposition on which they proceeded correct. Herr Kocker has, however, himself informed me differently; and his subsequent edition of the Chorales above referred to, shows clearly that his intention, and that of his associates, was merely to the effect that the congregation should sing the most simple tunes, harmonised as much as possible, in the common chord. This, no doubt, quite alters the question; and here it seems to me that everything must depend upon existing circumstances. That is

On the Chorale.

On the Chorale.
Under favourable circumstances the people should sing in harmony;

to say, if a community be intelligent and pious, observant of the sanctity of Sunday, and of good musical capability; if there be an abundance of exemplary clergymen, interested in the improvement of church music; if they be seconded by the advice and co-operation of thorough musicians, and if great diligence be bestowed upon the teaching of music in the national schools—all of which is at this moment the case, to a highly satisfactory degree in the kingdom of Wurtemberg—then good four-part congregational singing may be considered possible; and the attainment of such a result would greatly promote musical harmony, and call forth the powers of individual members of the congregation. But it is not everywhere that circumstances are so favourable. How many states and towns are there where spiritual authority is weak from utter laxity and indifference; how many churches where the priest will hear no voice but his own; how many places where absolutely nothing is done in earnest for musical schooling! Wherever this is the case, I would never advise that four-part singing should be attempted—at all events, not before the first steps have been taken. And here I would merely suggest that people should confine themselves to a selection of the best chorales, to be sung in unison with adequate organ accompaniment, and, next, that they should use their best endeavours to bring the melodies within such a compass as, by singing in octaves, would be, ordinarily, within the range of all voices; and thus avoid what has hitherto so often been the case, viz. for the basses and altos, or, again, the tenors and sopranos, to be half reduced to silence, or else forced to scream.

I have, in conclusion, one more observation to make, which is not aimed at any individual, but which, as a reproof of general incompetence, will certainly not be relished by the many to whom it will apply. It is to this effect, that a healthy condition of church music is hopeless, unless the organists be

On the Chorale. but, in the absence of favourable circumstances, in unison.

Necessity of a check upon organists.

On the Chorale.

under control; at least so long as we can point to but few such organists as Apel, Ett, Rinck, and Umbreit. For what have the organists brought us to? To nothing less than this,—that any one with the slightest knowledge of music but too often leaves the church in disgust with the flippancy and insipidity of the music. The prelude discomposes him for the chorale, the involved interlude goes far to distract him, and the concluding voluntary seems to have no other aim than to obliterate the sermon and all besides. Some allowance must of course be made for these delinquencies. Our organists are often in no position to get a sound musical training; they have, as a class, no more than the mechanical abilities of ordinary artisans; and lastly, if the emoluments of their office are but scanty, they are obliged to eke out a livelihood by mechanical instruction, in which the wants and wishes of the pupil are hindrances to the cultivation of art. But these are the very reasons why a congregation should say, "We want none of your pretended originality: all we ask of you is not to disturb our devotions, and not to scandalise us by making free with the church, and using it as a place for playing pranks." In truth, it passes comprehension how most of the clergy have quietly endured the misdemeanours of organists. It is of the first importance that this matter should be taken in hand; and the few organists of real talent cannot and ought not to demand that, in deference to them, the whole service should be at the mercy of the thousands who disconcert and annoy the best part of the congregation. Any organist, who has a high opinion of himself, can always let his light shine at organ recitals, or in any other way he pleases. Only let Divine Service proceed as it ought, simply and steadily in its appointed order, and not seem to be a recognised opportunity for every bad player to make experiments, and in airing his own profane conceits, to trample heedlessly upon all that is most sacred.

On the Chorale.

On the Chorale. Suggestion of an approved compilation of church-music for general use.

If I were now shortly to express my own wishes, I would say—make a collection of the best church-song, hearty, vigorous, and fervent; choose for this purpose the finest melodies that the old churches have left to us, including everything that in modern times masterly minds have added to them; and lastly, provide organists with a song-book in which everything shall be printed in full (for there are many who cannot readily play from a figured bass); and put into their hands also a collection of approved preludes and postludes, so that they can never waver or wander from the path. But do not do all this in any mean and paltry spirit, under the advice of inferior men. Rather treat the subject as a grave ecclesiastical question, requiring the aid of first-rate counsellors; and spend upon it at all events not less than what the Government contributes, perhaps in a single year, to a middling theatre. Then will a noble work have been accomplished that may bid defiance to time. Such works

PURITY IN MUSICAL ART.

On the Chorale.

are more needful to Lutherans than to others, if they would not end by making the temple a place where, in the name of reason and of art, little more is often to be heard than the poor crotchets of the clergy and their assistants.

Lastly, I would appeal to our Protestant congregations collectively. Agree upon a uniform chorale-book for all German Protestants, and so upon a work which, executed with the assistance of the first talent, would impart to your body, ever more and more, a happy consistency and unity. However, it is, I know, the very essence of the German spirit, that every man should abstain from troubling himself with his neighbour's concerns, and should stand supreme upon his own little patch of land. And so my appeal may as well at once be resolved into a sigh!

ON CHURCH MUSIC OTHER THAN THE CHORALE.

On Church Music other than the Chorale.

Natural fondness for good music.

THE popular mind, when left to itself, has a natural sympathy for music that truly and healthily reflects the genuine emotions of mankind; and there is no more effectual way of working upon it than by music of an elevating kind. Inasmuch then as an ordinary congregation can only be taught, as a rule, to sing simple hymns, the execution of sacred compositions of a higher type should be entrusted to finished singers; and thus it may seem as if angels were singing in the church, and the congregation may devoutly listen to that which their own numbers and unfitness disqualify them from executing themselves.

Gregory the Great's foundations.

This great idea was first carried into practical effect by Gregory the Great by the institution of numerous schools for singing; and for more than a thousand years afterwards every possible thing was done in the more enlightened Christian states towards this end. By degrees, however, people became indifferent, and church music (in which I do not here include the chorale) either wholly disappeared, or became undistinguishable from profane compositions, which, instead of ministering to piety, gave a place and a voice in the temple to secularism pure and simple. The very consideration of what becomes a church seems to have been, at last, utterly ignored. Nor is this difficult to understand. For religious earnestness is wont to wax cooler as mechanical skill increases. Nothing good could emanate from the majority of our musicians, because, if the truth be told, they are, generally speaking, utterly deficient in the higher education, poetical, philosophical, and historical, and because their aspirations go no farther than

On Church Music other than the Chorale.

Gradual secularisation of church music

as manipulative skill increased.

On Church Music other than the Chorale.

to have the opportunity of offering to us in church such pieces as they have happened to practice, or have themselves composed. And the accommodating ear of worldly-minded church-goers has everywhere encouraged the grossest abuses.

Happily there are still many who appreciate the value of real church music, or whose eyes could easily be opened to it. I shall proceed therefore, in a hopeful rather than a desponding spirit, humbly to contribute my mite towards so excellent an object.

The principle that ought to pervade church music is that of moderation.

The church is not the place where all that is enjoyable ought to be presented and enjoyed. It is nothing less than the place where man appears, as it were, in the sight of God, and before God, to refresh and to brace himself for his duties as a man, and where in His presence he pours forth his heart in grief, in penitence, in joy, and in supplication. Now as in God's presence all overweening self-confidence, all abject despair, is out of place, so neither in the church should there be any extravagance of jubilation nor any abandonment to grief. He, therefore, who desires to thank and praise God in all joyousness of heart, will express his gratitude, not with unbounded exultation, but with humble fervour; and he who is bowed down with sorrow, and who, outside the church's walls, would give himself up to melancholy and lamentation, must, within the church, and in the sight of God, take comfort to himself; not wringing his hands and running to and fro with sighs and moans, but, finding consolation through faith in a present God, he must, with patience and resignation, call on Heaven to witness and pity his grief. What it is that is becoming in the church may best be seen by reflecting for a moment on the duty of a preacher. In the theatre it is well enough for an actor of goodly mien to throw himself into all sorts of attitudes, and, according to the nature of the occasion, to bluster and to storm, to cringe and to crouch, to burn and to blaze in a transport

On Church Music other than the Chorale.

Example of a preacher.

On Church Music other than the Chorale.

of passion, to crack jokes, and, in short, to figure in characters taken from all countries and all times. But what is it that we expect in a priest, if we do not want the church turned into a theatre, but seek there for nourishment by God's word through the mouth of His minister? We should assuredly look for a sober, elevated, earnest address, delivered with manly force, with manly calmness and warmth, but without excitement, without parade and trickery—such, that is, as may lead us to forget the trifles of this world, and associate our thoughts with a better, where frivolity, hurtful passion, and consuming grief shall no more exist. Therefore a priest in the pulpit should not shout like a crier, who would intoxicate the people with joy at the news of a victory; should not rail at vice with the anger of a man who repels a personal insult; should not be all sugar and honey in his language; should not whine and weep, like frail humanity, which thinks itself deserted by God and man;

should not rant and bluster, nor use all kinds of gesture to express his emotions; should not despairingly wring his hands; should not even, if he can control human weakness, shed a single tear, however bitter be the misery he may have to deplore. This, and this only, is the demeanour that befits the church. For it is hers not to stimulate what is of the earth, not to fight with carnal weapons, but, by the suggestion of that Heaven, where all passion ceases, to soften and to elevate those who are subject to its influence.

On Church Music other than the Chorale.

This guiding principle, which should always be present to a clergyman's mind, must also be kept in view by all good musicians, who would take part in the Church's mission, and not use the sacred fabric merely as a place wherein all manner of sounds that may tickle the ear are to be heard. To ask what particular style of music belongs to the Church, is no more worthy of attention than to ask whether it is

On Church Music other than the Chorale.

Church music various in style, but uniform in sobriety of character.

open to a clergyman to declaim, to display emotion, and to enforce his declamation by gesticulations. All kinds of music are suitable for Church use, that do not of themselves call up purely secular associations, such as a waltz, or a gay Siciliano. Thus a Largo, an Adagio, a Grave, an Andante, an Allegro, a fugal or non-fugal piece, can all be performed in the Church, but should each and all be measured, serious, and dignified, should be throughout elevated and unimpassioned, and of such a tone that any preacher of note should be able to say, "This fine music is a fitting prelude to my discourse;" or "Following upon my sermon, it has stirred up the congregation to a lively sense of its import;" or again, as might in certain cases be well, "After such singing, my lips had better be closed, and the congregation left to their own silent devotions."

These considerations will readily commend themselves to, and be recognised as just by all unprejudiced persons; but I am well aware of the objection so often advanced by superficial minds, to the effect that church music of this character would become monotonous, and that genius casts off all restraint. But the answer to this (and it cannot be too often repeated) is, that genius no more despises strict rules than it despises hard work; and to affect an off-hand freedom from constraint is merely a stupid vanity, which lacks the ability necessary both for due submission and legitimate superiority to rule.

On Church Music other than the Chorale.

To the Church, as such, belongs only what is Church-like; and, if this be set forth with consummate skill, all purposes of devotion are fully served. Men must not forget that they are called upon to discharge various heavy duties in everyday life, and that the Church's office is not to minister to indolence, but to fortify energy. Its duty, therefore, will be to keep its proper bounds, and not attempt to enlarge its domain beyond what the Creator Himself intended. It is affectation to treat the inscrutable feelings and

The church essentially the place of religion.

On Church Music other than the Chorale.

aspirations, which in the Church raise the human soul aloft, as among the aims of every-day life. Whilst it is repulsive and unnatural for devoteeism, self-immolation, and monasticism, to try and stifle everything in life that Heaven has given to man for worldly enjoyment, it is not less repulsive when busybodies, because of the existence of abuses, assail all that is holy, and, from detestation of hypocrisy, are misled into dissociating religion from the Church, in order that the world may be secured from clerical extravagance.

A man of robust mind, who has found edification within the Church, will, on that account, throw himself afterwards into worldly concerns with all his heart; and, if he seek mental enjoyment, he will try either to qualify himself for great and lofty contemplations by diligent study of philosophy and poetry, or else to supply the necessary aliment to mere pleasure and enjoyment of life. In this way, then, there arise three styles of music:

Three great branches of music.

the church style, which is alone appropriated to devotional purposes; the oratorio style, which illustrates great and serious themes under human figures; and the operatic style, representing the world of sense and passion in a poetical form. As for a fourth style, in which all these elements are combined, passion surpasses itself, and every possible eccentricity is represented in music, it has no more place here than the cramp would have in a sound constitution.

Let us, then, leave to the Church all that properly belongs to it, and let us enhance it with all the resources of art, but not on that account neglect the other forms of music; on the contrary, let us attend to these more assiduously than to ecclesiastical music; for men's minds cannot long endure the region of the sublime, and in this world the demands of a busy life are more absorbing than the worship of the Almighty. But the lines of demarcation must not be confounded. Let those who pray say their prayers at church,

On Church Music other than the Chorale.

Church-music one thing; secular music another, equally or even more engrossing.

On Church Music other than the Chorale.

but not go on repeating them in the ball-room. Conversely, the graces of the ballet have no place among the solemnities of religion. I should consider it inexcusable for a single bar of a sacred work of Palestrina's to be introduced into an opera; but it would also be abominable to find in a Mass the least trace of the rich and ready fancy so peculiarly characteristic of the Figaro of Mozart. The judgment of the public can, indeed, always be imposed upon, if an abuse be consecrated by a plausible name. The blind followers of fashion are perfectly well satisfied that the music to the words "Liber scriptus proferetur," in Mozart's Requiem, should be of precisely the same character as that in his Figaro to the words of the melancholy female jester "Little Needle." But what cultivated person, in contemplating the Last Judgment, would like to have the song of the "Little Needle" put into his head, or to be reminded by the joke about the "Little Needle" of the terrors of the hell which might await him?

PURITY IN MUSICAL ART.

Turning now to the history of church music, a very short examination of the subject will show that the most recent times are the least deserving of commendation, and that, as with painting and architecture, so also with church music proper, the laurel crown is due pre-eminently to the great old masters. As early as the fifteenth and sixteenth centuries, the fine Church composers of the old German and Flemish school exhibit such power and such depth of feeling, together with such skill in the ingenious interweaving of voices, that one cannot sufficiently deplore their utter neglect at the present day. If, for instance, we compare Josquin's Stabat Mater (he died 1475) for five voices with the restless Stabat Mater of Pergolesi, or Christ's Seven Words by Senffel, Luther's contemporary, with those by Joseph Haydn, whose setting passes and repasses from one style into another, there can be no question on which side lies the most evidence of religious power. The last great master of the Flemish

On Church Music other than the Chorale.

Historical survey of ancient church-music.

Josquin.

Senffel.

Orlando di Lasso.

On Church Music other than the Chorale.

Palestrina.

school, Orlando di Lasso (Roland Lass, born 1520), in the numerous works which have come down to us, and which perhaps could not be contained in sixty folios, appears to our eyes a giant—as mighty, as tranquil, as serious, as tender, and as sympathetic, as the Church could desire. Close beside him comes, in Italy, Palestrina (Prænestinus), not less prolific in production, but perhaps profounder in conception. So perfect a master was he of the church tones, and of the treatment of the common chord, that there is, perhaps, more repose and inward satisfaction to be derived from his works than from those of any other author. These, printed long ago, are now, indeed, hardly to be procured in their original form, and it is difficult to get correct copies of them in manuscript. I would, however, call the attention of those who may at present be wholly ignorant of him to the following easily obtainable work, which appeared in Paris some years ago without date, and, unfortunately, with a good many misprints: "Collection des pièces de music religieuse qui s'exècutent tous les ans à Rome durant la semaine sainte," par A. Choron. In this collection are contained, amongst other things, Palestrina's Responsoria, which cannot be too highly praised, though the admirers of perpetual merrymaking and frivolity may perhaps see nothing in them. One must, indeed, realise, first of all, what it is that these dirges on Christ's Passion, sung on Good Friday night, convey; and if, after that, they be sung through by practised vocalists, the rest will quickly reveal itself; always supposing that the voices are good and pure, the necessary expression accurately observed, and the time duly kept, without hurrying on the one hand, or, on the other, setting out with the notion, common with Germans, that the prolonged notes of Italian composers must necessarily exhaust the breath. Special attention should be given to those portions of the Responsoria which are for three voices: their beauty, as

On Church Music other than the Chorale.

His "Responsoria."

On Church Music other than the Chorale.

a whole, is never so conspicuous as when rendered by first-rate female vocalists, one to each part. If they are awkwardly played, and the singing be harsh, wooden, and shrieky, then the mirror will undoubtedly be blurred; just as it is easy to ruin Goethe's "Iphigenia" by a bald recitation,—at all events, a thousand times easier than such a play as Kotzebue's " Misanthropy and Remorse."

But if Palestrina, who may fitly, in every sense, be compared with Homer, be in his way unsurpassed, and hence has given his name to the most perfect style of church music, yet it is a mistake to regard him as at once the beginning and the end of the great church style. The title of inventor here belongs, without doubt, rather to the earlier German and Flemish musicians, among which last must be named Palestrina's master Goudimel. Thus there stand beside Palestrina, and, generally, comparable to him, the Flemish Lasso and the Spanish Morales, whose " Lamentabatur Jacobus" was declared by Father

Morales.

Martini, the first historian of music, to be the most perfect composition in existence. Close upon Palestrina, again, follow two great church composers, who can hardly be said to be entirely formed by his writings; the German Hänel or Handl (James Gallus, born 1550), and the Spanish Tomaso Ludovico Vittoria (born 1560), the latter of whom united most happily the devotional spirit with the fire of the Spanish character. After these come, in Italy, many more authors, who laboured, if not in all cases, yet frequently, with success in the severe style; in particular Allegri, Alessandro Scarlatti, who wrote some two hundred masses, and was highly esteemed both by Handel and Hasse; Bai, Lotti (Hasse's favourite), Durante Bernabei, Father Martini, and the occasionally admirable yet unequal Jomelli, as well as several others, whose works I have seen, and many more of whom I know, so far, only by hearsay.

Meantime, after Palestrina there soon sprang up a tendency towards what I have

On Church Music other than the Chorale.

Vittoria.

Scarlatti.

Lotti.

Jomelli.

Tendency, after Palestrina, towards the Oratorio style

On Church Music other than the Chorale.

not unnatural.

Caldara, Durante, Leo, etc.

before called the Oratorio style, which was everywhere introduced into the churches; the Sistine Chapel excepted, which has never quite abandoned ecclesiastical severity, and so has stood, in regard to music, as a rock in the sea. The progress of this tendency is not at all difficult to understand. For it is precisely the Sublime that soonest loses its hold on the generality of people; and, as in old times musicians had to do without concert-rooms and theatres, it was not unnatural that they should use the church to give free scope to their inventive faculties; a consideration which also explains the growth of sacred comedy in former times within the cloisters. The number of lively composers who now arose is very large; and among them deserve special mention—judging always by the quality of most of their works—Caldara (born 1668), Marcello (born 1680), Durante (born 1693), Leonardo Leo (born 1694), Valotti (born 1705), and Pergolesi (born 1707). But it must be said to their credit that, even in their most animated pieces, there are abundant indications of their love for the severe style; that they seldom or never stray into the frivolities of opera; and that they sought somehow to combine the severe and the beautiful, and thus to satisfy at once the devotional and the inventive spirit. We need only take as an instance Leo's celebrated Miserere for eight voices. It is not indeed to be compared in many respects with a Miserere of Lasso's, Allegri's, Bai's, or one of Lotti's great Misereres. But how dignified is it, as a whole, in character; how delicately suggestive of true religious feeling the inweaving of Gregorian melody; and if the "Cor mundum crea in me" be sung with perfect nicety, our thoughts can only turn to the sweet angels of heaven, not to the syrens of the stage. Moreover, in these animated productions of the higher sacred Italian composers, all defects are generally compensated by this—that all flows from a genuine inspiration, and is written

On Church Music other than the Chorale.

The spirit of the older style still retained.

On Church Music other than the Chorale.

Oratorio the chosen field of Handel and Bach,

who always observed its proper limits.

with a freedom of spirit and a purity of taste that may well make a man glad to forget for the moment the sanctity of the spot where he is standing.

This Oratorio style is the one to which the best German masters of the last generation—viz. Handel, Sebastian Bach, Hasse, and Graun—have, in their greater efforts, almost exclusively devoted themselves; partly because of the recent condition of German churches, and partly, as cannot be denied, because genius has far more scope when untrammelled, and independent of ecclesiastical obligations. But these authors have never allowed their oratorios to travel away into opera; and, in truth, Handel's strict fidelity to the union of the solemn and the spirited elements, whilst at the same time he was doing, and was obliged to do, so much for the opera, deserves the highest admiration.

But what shall I say of the works which have appeared within the last fifty years in the category of the Church and Oratorio styles? I state it once more as my conviction that the Church style is almost utterly lost; the Oratorio style has almost universally passed into the Operatic; the Operatic into a wild and silly extravagance: and such is the medley which it is often attempted to introduce into the church. I cannot stop here to mention exceptions which have to be made. Many German composers now living, whom I scruple to name, know perfectly well, from my opinion of their works, that I am not one of those who are blind to everything not ancient, and who cast aside unregarded everything new, because it is new. But if I were to ask those who value real merit, and have an adequate knowledge of modern music, whether, in their conscientious opinion, all the many works which, through fashion or through the personal influence of their authors or publishers, or from local circumstances, have obtained a sort of prominence, exhibit collectively as much force of genius and depth

On Church Music other than the Chorale.

Low state of modern music, as seen in the Church, the Oratorio, and the Opera.

of feeling as Handel's Messiah alone, I cannot think that any serious-minded and intelligent person would consider my question an impertinent one. Put it to the proof with good and practised singers. You will find it difficult to bring forward any modern piece after Handel's Messiah, worthily rendered, that does not suffer by comparison. But the finer pieces of Palestrina, Lasso, Vittoria, Caldara, Marcello, Lotti, and Durante, will never lose their charm, preceded though they be by all the best selections from Handel and Sebastian Bach.

The admirers of the modern school feel themselves, indeed, much aggrieved by conclusions like these; and it is, in particular, usually regarded as an atrocious libel if no exception be made in favour of Haydn's and Mozart's Masses. But it is pretty well known that neither of these masters set any value upon their sacred compositions, as such,—that Mozart himself laughed at the Masses which necessity compelled him to write, and that Joseph Haydn unhesitatingly yielded the palm in the true church style to his brother Michael. I readily allow that these Masses are well calculated to please, possessing as they do much flow and elegance; but I contend that their prevailing character is sensuous, secular, in a word, wholly unworthy, on the highest grounds, of the church; and that, within the walls of a church they can give no pleasure to a devout mind, acquainted with the older masterpieces of the true church style, or even with the finer examples of oratorio. It is the same as with the church fabrics themselves. We build now-a-days plenty of smart edifices, variously coloured and ornamented, but not one capable of overwhelming us with wonder and reverence, such as the portico of Strasburg Cathedral. *[On Church Music other than the Chorale.]*

I must, however, notice the retort sometimes made in haughty tones by many so-called musicians about the glory of advancing with the spirit of the age, and about the *[The plea of progress and modern improvement.]*

On Church Music other than the Chorale.

gigantic strides that art has of late made. Talk of this kind has already, in some instances, brought us to this—that the splendid symphonies of our countryman Joseph Haydn are shelved as obsolete or obsolescent stuff; and even Mozart's pieces are taken much faster than he himself intended; just as if the disquietude which armaments, expresses, and steamboats have brought upon Europe, must also invade the æsthetic domain of art.

The supposed superiority of modern music no reason for neglecting ancient.

Admitting, for a moment, the superiority of the modern school, why, I would ask, should music alone be stricken with poverty and narrowness of spirit? Go where you will, it is an acknowledged necessity not only to live in the present, but to make the works of all ages one's own, as being the best way to obtain instruction, and because, as a rule, every period has its characteristic excellence. Then why is music, forsooth, to be an exception? It is a remarkable feature of our age, that as regards the pleasures, not only of the mind, but like-

PURITY IN MUSICAL ART.

wise of the table, we are unable properly to digest our food, quickly become sated with each dish, and yet never tire of sweetmeats. This may be called the spirit of progress. Yet ought we, after all, to be ashamed of going back to our great ancestors, and borrowing from them something of their repose, their solidity, their strength, and therewith something of the beautiful and lovely spirit which has given us so many restful, cheering, and refreshing melodies? *On Church Music other than the Chorale.*

That the art in its practical aspect has of late made enormous strides is certain; especially the art of instrumentation; the art of pourtraying by music purely sensible objects and far-fetched fancies; the art of painting tone-pictures, and representing natural phenomena; the art of executing a shake with a dying breath, and, above all, the art of linking music to everything foreign to it. On the other hand, justice requires us thankfully to confess that, in the progress of the art, much has been done for sound forms of *Improvement in certain ways undeniable.*

PURITY IN MUSICAL ART.

On Church Music other than the Chorale.

Palestrina not to be compared with Handel or Bach as a fugue writer.

music. For instance, I should consider it childish to think for a moment of comparing Palestrina's "Missa ad Fugam," lately published in Paris, with one of Handel's or Sebastian Bach's great fugues. But let us not on that account forget the infinite amount of trash and ugliness that modern taste has at the same time brought into circulation; how, for instance, the fugue, founded on certain easily acquired rules, has become a miserable refuge for the inaptitude of hundreds; and how many new theories have been trumped up (*e.g.*, on consecutive fifths) by modern harmonists, against which protests founded on ancient models are even now raised.

Every reason to look for superlative merit in the early composers

It must be acknowledged by any man of intelligence and impartiality that ancient masters were as well acquainted with the essence of musical art as are modern masters; they were acquainted therefore with melody (as is best proved by their incomparable chorales) as well as harmony; and this last was studied by them, the framers of all the principal rules still in force, more profoundly and more assiduously than it is now, as many old theoretical treatises will show. The departments of music to which they gave all their attention were, therefore, brought to the highest state of cultivation; and indeed it would be surprising if the fifteenth and sixteenth centuries, which teemed with artists of genius, had produced nothing remarkable in music alone. We read of Correggio, that in his last sleep before death, he dreamt with rapture that he had met Palestrina in heaven; and we may suppose, therefore, that the masterpieces of the great musician had inspired the gifted painter, while here below, with reverence for their author. Let our musical egotists, who often have to affect a pitiable disdain to conceal their own destitution, gladly avow what no discerning eye can fail to see. We censure what we have never seen; we refuse to be introduced to what we can with difficulty comprehend and

On Church Music other than the Chorale.

No excuse for our ignorance of their works.

On Church Music other than the Chorale.

perform; moreover, both money and patience are lacking to procure and study but half a score of the thousands and thousands of ancient works which have come down to us.

The highest works are due to genius rather than to cultivation;

A work, to be classical, must always, according to universal understanding, be the issue of a great spirit, evincing the free action of a powerful mind; and, by such a right, it belongs to all time, so long as genius is had in honour. Plato can never, any more than Shakespeare, cease to please from lapse of years; and Mozart, as a true genius, would have been a brilliant example of any style, whether he had lived earlier or later, among Alpine goatherds, or in a cloister, or in regal luxury. Increased cultivation may indeed

and often possess more force than polish.

produce great improvement as regards polish; but strength and vigour must ever well from the fountain-head of genius; and this vigour, from the very fact of its deficiency in polish, usually exhibits a quality and freshness that a fully-developed condition of art cannot give but may very easily destroy.

For this reason I readily grant that if those who are always raising petty objections obstinately persist in shutting their eyes, and refuse to wean themselves from the hysterical and sensational fashion of the day, they must leave the works of the great old masters of the church and oratorio style alone. No image can be clearly reflected in muddy water, and Raphael's angels are as nothing to dazzled eyes. But if they would only brace themselves in earnest for those works, choose the hours when they feel calm, serene, and amenable to impressions that are not sensational, and do their best to secure a first-rate execution, they will find in them soon enough a source of heavenly satisfaction, and will see that those who now assume the part of censors have nothing to complain of but their own obtuseness and bigotry.

On Church Music other than the Chorale. They are not likely to be appreciated by those who abandon themselves to the sensuous music of the day.

Inferior composers there have been, certainly, in former times, in Italy as well as in Germany; and it must be confessed that the old opera suffers not unfrequently from a

Stiffness of old opera music as compared with modern.

On Church Music other than the Chorale.

Reversal of relations of the church and the stage.

certain stiffness, which the light and frivolous manner now in favour has altogether obliterated. The fact is, that just as at first the old church music, being the most ancient type of music, often exercised an influence upon the stage, so now, conversely, the sensuousness of the modern stage is like to react upon the church; and I leave it to the high and mighty critics of the day to try and answer the question, whether it be as repulsive to witness the somewhat awkward performance of a nun, who has deserted the convent for the stage, as to see the part of the Holy Mother taken by a giddy actress in a church.

Intrinsic merits of the old opera.

But what, it will be asked, would be a fair estimate of the old opera? Polished in a particular way, and complete in itself like the modern opera, it certainly was not. But if we were to search out and to reckon up, by way of comparison, all that is meritorious and striking in the earlier operatic works, how much is there from the modern *repertoire* that could weigh in the other scale, and how many of the pieces now in favour would have to shrink abashed into the background! We need only look into Handel's operas to find the most admirable passages. Forkel has, I know, somewhere ventured the remark —quite in accordance with his views—that it is not easy to find any air of Handel's fit to do duty at the present day; and this has been repeated by others, who certainly knew less of Handel than Forkel. But a more ill-considered statement could scarcely be made. Having a tolerably accurate knowledge of Handel's works, I am confident that I could produce from them a long list of airs, chiefly for soprano, alto, and bass, that could not fail to delight any one amenable to the charms of music, evincing, as they do, a purity, a tenderness, and a power of sympathy, not often to be found in modern composers.

<small>*On Church Music other than the Chorale.*

Handel's operas full of beauties.</small>

ON POPULAR MELODIES.

On Popular Melodies.
The virtues of childhood.

THE inclination of an educated man will and must be, principally, to seek instruction and entertainment from intercourse with all who are distinguished for their learning. Still he ought not to lose all relish for the charm of innocence; for culture, as we see it in the world, is by no means always a true development of nature; and, in this sense, it is quite possible for an educated man to rank beneath a child. It is said of children in the Gospel that of them is the kingdom of God; and herein lies an eminent truth. Perfect openness, sincerity, and truthfulness are the noblest traits of the human character. But education, and the circumstances of life, generally make a man more or less close, calculating, disingenuous, and deceitful;

PURITY IN MUSICAL ART.

whereas a child stands before us with his virtues and his faults, a fresh and virgin specimen of nature's handiwork. Therefore he who knows not the child knows not the man; and Rousseau says, with great truth, that the time of youth—that is to say, of youth's frank intercourse—is the time which a wise man ought to study.

These remarks are also applicable to music. The greatest treat that any man of mind can have in music is, undoubtedly, a perfect work of art. But how easy is it for art to become unnatural; how easy for a thing to be overdone; and how often do we find music, laboriously composed by mere artifice, uninspired by any real spontaneous emotion, and exciting, therefore, at best admiration, but not love! It may be asserted, without exaggeration, that one half of our music is destitute of the natural element; a species of mathematics without a spark of life; a mere display for the honour and glory of nimble fingers; and such a compound of unwholesome in-

On Popular Melodies.

Art a supreme delight, yet liable to failure.

gredients, that it may seriously be asked whether it does not do us more harm than good. On the other hand, all the songs that emanate from the people themselves, or are adopted by them and preserved as favourites, are, as a rule, pure and clear in character, like that of a child. Such songs almost invariably re-echo the emotions of vigorous, unperverted minds, and for that very reason have in various ways quite a peculiar value from their connection with great national events; and, dating from times when nations had all the innocence and freshness of youth, they seize with irresistible force upon minds which, however much warped, are still alive to true and genuine impulse.

For this reason, I hold the study of popular songs—by which I do not mean ephemeral street ballads, but such songs as live and thrive in the popular mind—to be of the utmost importance. But if we wish to do real service to art in reference to them, it is necessary to look all around, and not confine

Sidenotes:
On Popular Melodies.
Popular airs the artless expressions of national youth.

Interest attaching to the study of the popular songs of all countries.

PURITY IN MUSICAL ART. 69

ourselves to the songs that are popular in our own land, but to take all the world into our survey, and endeavour to read each nation's character in their songs. We travel, and read accounts of travels, to gain an idea of each country's peculiarities; and why should music, often so intensely characteristic, be left unnoticed? " If Goethe, after writing his "Goetz," had done no more than give us other pictures of old German character, he would have done a thing worthy of all honour. But he has earned the title of the Prince of our poets from the very fact that in his "Iphigenia" he has also been able to transport us into the fairest times of Greece, as in his "East-and-West Divan" he has taken us into Persia and India, and because in his "Faust" he belongs to the universal world of genius."

A man who, in bye-hours, resorts to the bright and cheerful domain of art for recreation from severe professional labour, is wont to do so with a keener relish than the regular

On Popular Melodies.

Advantage of the amateur.

On Popular Melodies.

artist, who has his main occupation therein. In other words, the sauce when taken in small quantities is usually more savoury than when taken in spoonfuls. And so I have spared no pains in searching for materials to satisfy my curiosity in connection with this

Difficulties in the way of a collector.

subject. But, though I have to a considerable extent succeeded, I am still far from the desired end. Any one who sets about historical investigations in music has the misfortune to find himself at a disadvantage. The generality of musicians entirely decline to listen to history. From the few well-read musicians and amateurs much could indeed be obtained; but here again the prospect is often a discouraging one. Collectors are, as a rule, far readier to take than to give; they are wonderfully reserved and forgetful, and are only too glad to leave inquirers to their own resources, with a tacit "Physician, heal thyself!" Others will undertake anything, but oftentimes with no better result than good wishes. By degrees, however, and by the active assistance of some generous friends, I have collected a number of popular airs, on which I set much value. Others may possess, or be acquainted with many more; but I am sure there are many who have and know less. I may proceed, therefore, frankly to specify those I have and know, hoping that those who are richer than myself may supply my deficiencies out of their abundance, or may, at least, be so kind as to put me on the right track if I go astray; in return for which I shall gladly place at their disposal any duplicates I may happen to possess.

On Popular Melodies.

Our curiosity as to national songs must naturally cause us first to look out for any that may have been preserved from the earliest times. But though some theoretical treatises of the era before Christ have reached us, we are yet without such good specimens as are necessary for the object in view.

The old Israelitish melodies would possess for us the deepest interest, inasmuch as they probably exercised a direct influence upon

Ineffectual search for Israelitish songs.

On Popular Melodies.

the first Christian churches. Supposing that Judaism obstinately adheres to ancient customs, I made diligent inquiries in the German synagogues; but quite in vain. The sole piece communicated to me, which I was able to trace with certainty, was a recitative from an opera of Mozart! Marcello is known to have made similar investigations, and several of the intonations used by German and Spanish Jews, given in his great Collection of Psalms, have a peculiar Oriental character. But, unfortunately, he does not give his authorities; nor is there any better foundation for the very interesting work recently translated from the English—" Collection of National Hebrew Melodies, with accompanying words by Lord Byron," published by G. K. R. Kretshmer, at the Magazine for art, geography, and music in Berlin. No one will deny that much of its contents is to be traced to modern sources, particularly in the accompaniments.

PURITY IN MUSICAL ART.

Genuine old Greek songs would, presumably, prove as interesting as Pindar; but they are not to be found. Burney, in his treatise on ancient music, has, indeed, given us some songs taken from a Parisian MS., which really seem referable to ancient Greece, and which have since been several times published, as, for instance, in Forkel's History. They are obviously highly original, for which reason our great philologist, Wolf, was beyond measure delighted with them. But the inferences deducible from them as to the general character of Grecian music are very slender indeed. It is likely enough that some traditions of old times may still be extant among the modern Greeks. But I know of no one who has turned his attention in this direction, except Sulzer in his History of Transalpine Dacia (Vienna, 1781-1782, 2 vols. 8vo), to which work some notable modern Greek songs are appended. They are also interesting as distinctly recalling some of the tunes of the Russo-Greek Church.

On Popular Melodies. Scant remains of Greek music.

On Popular Melodies.

Airs of the Troubadours, Minnesänger, Meistersänger.

Passing on to the period after Christ, the airs of the Troubadours and Minnesingers, as well as of the people called Meistersingers, are of the highest importance in reference to national melodies. But just where all ought to be clear, had we always had historical students of music, everything seems as yet in utter obscurity. The specimens given by Busby in his history, especially the fine song of Ganelem on the death of King Richard I. of England, prompted me to renew my researches. But I met with nothing but barren quotations, such as Forkel usually gives. It was only by accident that I got hold of some capital melodies from a very old Nuremberg MS., and again, from "Elips von Zesen's Dramatic Vale of Roses and Lilies," Hamburg, 1670, 8vo, in which there are some highly original things; and, lastly, from the following little publications:—" A pocket Manual full of choice and lovely popular songs," Berlin, 1777; and " Melodies to a collection of German, Flemish, and

French popular songs," edited by Büsching and Von der Hagen, and published in Berlin by Braun. But they do not contain much that is attractive; and, as with many poems that pass for old, one can never be sure that unscrupulous editors may not have interpolated their own handiwork. The most original matter, and of true German growth, may be found in the work entitled " Popular Songs of Austria, with their airs, collected and edited by Ziska and Schottky," Pesth, 1819. Various editions of Swiss songs should also be mentioned. They are known to all musicsellers, and are to be seen in Switzerland unfolded in the windows of bookshops. It is highly probable that some new light may be thrown on the Troubadour songs. On the strength of the well-known story that Queen Christina of Sweden made a collection of them, and that the MS. was in the Vatican Library, I begged an accomplished friend of mine in Rome to make an examination. But I received poor comfort

On Popular Melodies.

Austrian Melodies.

Swiss Melodies.

Troubadour songs.

On Popular Melodies.

Difficulty of deciphering these last.

British Airs.

in the news that the MS. contained only words, and no notes. I then had recourse, through another friend, to Raynouard, editor of the "Choix des Poesies des Troubadours." He placed in my hands a song with accompanying notes, adding that he possessed many of them, and would send them all to me, if I could decipher this one. This, alas! I was not skilful enough to do, and so handed the treasure over to a friend more competent than myself. He had no sooner got it than he lost it; and after this I had never time or opportunity to revert to the subject. I merely drop a hint to all true musicians to make Paris the ground for further search. It is not too much to say that real lovers of fine music would gladly part with a thousand variations, sonatas, and other musical effusions of the day, if the old works of art in their genuineness and integrity could be procured in exchange.

The English have taken much pains with their national songs; yet in the new editions the words are quite modernised, and new words frequently assigned to the airs. The best notice of the subject is to be found in the preface of the following work, containing the old Scottish songs without accompaniment: "Scotch Songs," in 2 vols. 8vo, published by Johnson, London, 1794. Later, again, there came out, without date, in London, beautifully printed in fourteen small folios, and prettily got up with illustrations, a complete collection of Scotch, Irish, and Welsh popular songs, enriched with several modern additions, and with a pianoforte accompaniment, comprising preludes, postludes, and interludes, in which Pleyel, Joseph Haydn, Kotzeluch, and Beethoven, had a hand. The titles of these—I am sorry to say expensive—works are, "A Select Collection of original Scottish airs for the voice," etc. : London, printed by Preston, 4 vols. folio; "A Selection of Irish Melodies," *ibid.* 8 vols. folio; "A Selection of Welsh Melodies," 2 vols. folio. These three works,—the

On Popular Melodies.

On Popular Melodies.

two last especially,—comprise, together (as might be expected) with much that is insignificant, an extensive series of the most tender, vigorous, and animated pieces, which quite captivated no less a person than Joseph Haydn.

Russian Airs.

The national songs of Russia, some of which have quite an Oriental flavour, are most remarkable. My knowledge of them is derived from the following works, to which a pianoforte accompaniment is added—I give the titles in Russian, with Latin characters: —" Pjesennik' ulu polroe sobranie starüch'u nobüch' Rossiisküch' narodnüch'" (Petersburgh, without date, 8vo); "Sobranie Russküch' narodnüch' pjesen' s' üch golosami, poloschennüch na musüku Iwanom' Pratschem':" Petersburgh, 1806, 2 vols. 4to.

Danish Airs.

Very fine old Danish airs are to be found, though without accompaniment, in the fifth volume of "Danske's Melodies from the Middle Ages," by Nierup and Rahbek: Copenhagen, 1814, 8vo.

PURITY IN MUSICAL ART.

Some very interesting old Swedish and Finnish songs are given, in part with an accompaniment added, in Geyer and Afzelius's "Swedish Popular Melodies:" Stockholm, 1814-1816, 3 vols. 8vo; and in Schötter's "Finnish Runes:" Upsala, 1819, 8vo.

On Popular Melodies.
Swedish and Finnish Airs.

I know of no printed edition of the popular songs of Italy; but I possess a good number of them in MS. Every one knows how enchanting some of them are.

Italian Airs.

The national songs of Spain I know only from the lips of Spanish female singers. All my efforts to obtain the best of them, whether in print or MS., from Madrid have been fruitless. Considering the gifts and the uncommon fire of the Spanish people, recollecting only their Morales and their Vittoria, and seeing that in former times nearly all the best singers of the Papal Chapel were Spaniards, one can hardly doubt that any person who had the will and the opportunity to search for popular melodies in Spain,

Spanish Airs.

On Popular Melodies.

Brazilian Airs.

would be sure to find things of remarkable and possibly transcendent merit.

Popular songs of Brazil, and songs and dances of the American Indians, appeared some years ago in an appendix to Spix's and Martin's "Travels in Brazil." But the Brazilian songs seem to have their origin in modern Portuguese operas. The popular influence of the opera is now-a-days such, that any one who does not observe the landmarks of history is almost certain to be deluded. In the summer of 1824 I got together the best female vocalists among the Alps of the Bernese Oberland, that I might enjoy the old melodies; but, lo and behold! one of the first pieces was—a new operatic air.

Indian Airs.

Sir William Jones, in his work on Indian music, has given us Indian, Persian, and Moorish songs, often without words, and always without accompaniment. An assortment of them, chosen at random, together with much accessory matter, has recently appeared in London, very showily, but often very poorly arranged, under the title, "Indian Melodies, arranged for the Voice and Pianoforte in Songs, Duets, and Glees, by C. E. Horn," 1 vol. folio.

On Popular Melodies.

There is also a good deal in the narratives of various travellers that deserves attention. But pains must always be taken to collect the spirit of each particular piece; and this is often difficult to do, especially when the key is doubtful; from which cause it is not uncommon to this day for the finest pieces to be quite spoilt by false harmonisation, and particularly from not understanding the superscribed thirds and fifths.

Foreign airs not always easy to appreciate.

Often have I wished that I were qualified, as a musical theorist and thorough linguist, to devote my whole time, but for a single year, to an arrangement of the best songs of all countries. I should soon obtain a collection which would give pleasure alike to educated and uneducated. But I leave it to those who have more knowledge, talent, time,

Value of a compilation of National Melodies.

On Popular Melodies. and opportunity, to bethink themselves seriously of a compilation of this kind. A return to simple and natural ways is daily becoming in every respect more and more necessary. Music, in truth, can boast but little of having escaped all share in the false tendencies of the age.

ON THE INSTRUCTION TO BE DERIVED FROM GOOD MODELS.

KANT says somewhere of mathematics, that they are but a poor science, because an unfit subject for philosophy. The same might almost be said of music, as regards its influence upon education at the present day. Execution and flourish we have everywhere; mountains of amazing difficulty; a plethora of notes in place of completeness and perspicuity; but, apart from the satisfaction of vanity or professional whims, little of comfort or pleasure; so that our good maidens, when they get a hearth of their own, and can settle down there, gladly throw to the winds all the so-called art they have learnt.

No art is without a living principle; and

On the Instruction to be derived from good Models.

Music, as now practised, abounds in difficulties, but is deficient in zest.

A living principle essential to Music, as to other arts.

On the Instruction to be derived from good Models.

The essence of Music is expression of feeling, not conformity to rule.

this may be easily found in music, by going back to the point where it took its rise, and became a want. In other words, music is, in its essence, nothing but, as it were, the overflowing of emotion—of mental ecstasy—in sound; and, whenever a piece of music answers to this description, it will never fail to move and enchant all unprejudiced minds, barring, of course, that exceptional class that have no sense of tune, and to whom music is a sealed book, like a statue to a blind man. Music requires, indeed, a code of rules, just as poesy requires a system of versification. But true excellence in a musical work can no more follow from conformity to rule, or from artifice, than it can in a poem from regularity of versification. A composition that appeals in no way to the heart, or which jars upon the feelings, can never be anything better than a practice-piece, however much in favour it may be with the admirers of bravura. A Dutch preacher succeeded, after thirty years' labour, in engraving with a pin a whole troop of soldiers upon a small coin; but I imagine that no one would hang up the coin as a worthy companion to a Madonna of Raphael. I freely grant that music may be really embellished by art, just as a fair maiden by dress. But the incidents must not be mistaken for the essence. The divinity of music is only revealed when it transports us into an ideal state of being; and the composer who cannot do this for us is, so far, a mere hewer of wood and drawer of water.

On the Instruction to be derived from good Models.

If, in judging of musical works, we seek for a common point of comparison in men's sentiments and instincts (such instincts, that is, as are a worthy subject-matter for art, and so may serve in some sort as a standard), we find a hopeless difficulty in attempting to reduce all classes of people to one common measure. For, as to instincts, every one has his own standard, often so interwoven with the whole nature of the individual, that no human power can prevail against it.

Music pleases according to accidental tastes and habits.

On the Instruction to be derived from good Models.

Take, first, the untamed savage, who reproduces in his songs and in his dress his highest idea, brute force; and then go on through innumerable gradations, to the languid heroine of romance, who recoils from all that is vigorous and pure;—where, among these, is the talent of the musician to find a proper basis for its creations? Take into account, too, the fanciful interpretations, and the semi-philosophical, semi-poetical meanings perpetually attributed to plain things in the present day; and that precious indolence which refuses to pursue or acquire anything solid, and so tries to deafen us by rude noise. I know persons who have studied, or pretended to study, but twenty or thirty modern pieces, but who imagine that they have thereby rendered themselves such complete masters of musical science that they turn a deaf ear to everything else, loudly talk the silliest nonsense, and cannot refrain from a smile of commiseration if any hint is dropped of Lasso, Palestrina, Morales, Lotti, and

Durante,—not to mention Luther's favourite, Senffel, whose name, moreover, will not be relished by their dainty palates.*

On the Instruction to be derived from good Models.

Formerly, when I received the first impressions of those great compositions, which will ever possess for me a life-long charm, I used to be impatient if others would not understand them, and could listen to nothing but the fragments they had in their heads. Now that experience has made me wiser, though I still feel something of the same kind, yet I sit still calmly and civilly, and recall to myself the story of a minister of state coming to Frederick the Great, and depreciating Homer, Virgil, Plato, and such like, while praising to the skies the first catcher of herrings; whereupon the king merely remarked, " I suppose you are very fond of herrings!" In truth, there can hardly be a more erroneous idea than that music can make a man. It can do no more than respond to what good a man may have in him, or else rouse some-

Bad taste must be borne with.

Music cannot make a man; it presupposes a healthy nature.

* Senf—*Angl.* Mustard.

On the Instruction to be derived from good Models.

thing that lies dormant in him. A cold, vain man, of contracted ideas, and debased affections, will never appreciate a grand piece of music; and if there be added to this a quarrelsome temper, or the usual professional conceit, as disagreeable as it is barren; or if—lowest of all conditions—when he attends a concert, his small soul has no room for aught beside the two or three pieces he has at some former time acquired, or has heard in his own beloved town, then, indeed, are all attempts at conversion idle.

Musical taste not to be imparted by Lectures.

Words and theories can no more enlighten the mind on the subject of music than can abstract principles of painting give a correct eye for colour. Those who talk of musical theorems are much addicted to descriptions, but are not sensible of the small effect produced by them. The human frame admits of description much more easily than an invisible note; and yet no one ever found it on inspection the same as he had imagined from description. But there is one great resource always open to the lover of good music, which must always rank as the best means for influencing taste and feeling; and this is the information and improvement derivable from classical models. However much a mistaken culture may warp and narrow most people's minds, it is certain that, if the taste is not utterly depraved nor ruined by artificialism, the better element is not wholly quenched, but, at the worst, only slumbers; and it will be found, as a rule, that the study of great models leads in the end to a just estimate of their worth. I have known passionate admirers of Kotzebue, but not one who remained of the same mind after attentively reading Shakespeare; and I used myself, fifteen years ago, to admire musical works, which now, with more historical knowledge, I scarcely care to look at. And such has been the case with others. It is hardly to be believed how speedily the influence of good examples is felt. I have more than once found one-sided people,

On the Instruction to be derived from good Models.

Classical authors the great teachers.

Personal experience of their influence.

On the Instruction to be derived from good Models.

who, from certain hybrid pieces, had conceived a great idea of certain modern composers. These pieces I had sung, having previously selected others by Lasso, Palestrina, Lotti, and Sebastian Bach, not exactly of a profound, but of pure and dignified character. The question was decided in a moment, and never did a similar experiment fail. What actually occurred, to my great satisfaction, was this: a young man came to me with his head full of wrong ideas, and, after listening to a Mass of Lotti's, exclaimed in ecstasy, "This evening I can bear ill-will to no man." Effects like this might often be noticed, if people wished for them, and were not content to cling with miserable obstinacy to the approved fashion of the day.

Works of less than the highest order have their legitimate use.

Works of mediocrity may have their place, provided only they be healthy and unaffected. Men are not disposed to be reading the Psalms, or Homer, every hour of the day. They crave variety to entertain them, and help them to pass the time without mental strain. A large portion of the public have neither taste nor capacity for anything beyond mediocrity. Hence I should not be disposed to criticise several songs now in fashion so severely as some connoisseurs may have done. I merely ask those who can only understand and enjoy indifferent music, to abstain from pronouncing upon works of real genius, and not to expect masterpieces like the Merry Wives of Windsor and Don Quixote from the same pen as "The Provincials" and "The Bard with the Iron Helm."*

On the Instruction to be derived from good Models.

In all this, I wish to warn people against a certain prejudice and narrowness, which meets one at every turn. For instance, if an amateur has mastered certain pieces, and takes due pleasure in them, he is apt, for that very reason, to think them beautiful, nay, more beautiful than all others; and he will very likely take umbrage, if it be hinted that there are other more beautiful—far

Superficial knowledge likely to mislead.

* By Kotzebue.

On the Instruction to be derived from good Models.

Good judgment in Music accrues by degrees, and from mature experience.

more beautiful—pieces. Such narrowness is mischievous in the highest degree. Music is essentially a matter of taste, but taste is first formed by slow degrees. Test it by the analogy of Painting and Poetry. What pleased the boy fails to satisfy the young man; what transported the young man the grown man often finds empty and defective. By such tests and comparisons we shall at last realise what is truly classical, and attain therein a happy repose, because its characteristic is that it can be enjoyed over and over again, and rather gains than loses by repetition. So, if it be that heretofore a person has had but little knowledge, no one can say whither an educated taste may not lead him; and it is therefore mere indolence, or want of spirit, on the strength of the known to presume on the unknown, and doggedly refuse to go further. There can be wisdom in such conduct only when any one possessed of complete knowledge puts into your hands that which is of the highest and most unquestionable merit, and in this way excludes all that is indifferent and worthless—a most valuable educational help. But, in the case of music, it is seldom that such a mentor is at hand, and then many trials must be made before the object is attained. Ambition is not indeed disposed to confess its errors. But what harm can there be in saying, "What a simpleton I was up to such and such a year!" if you are happily able to add the reflection, "But how knowing I am now!"

On the Instruction to be derived from good Models.

ON EFFECT.

On Effect.

The production of effect not a proper function of art.

THOROUGH-GOING admirers of modern art plume themselves particularly on their efforts to produce what is termed effect, as a striking feature in the modern practice of music. But it is precisely here that the lover of true art finds most cause for censure. For this much-loved effect either betrays the hand of a bad workman, or else of a coward who is for serving and pleasing everybody. Nature does not go by fits and starts; nor do our emotions, in their normal state, oscillate irregularly, or exceed their bounds. Thus, your favourite symphonies, fantasias, pot-pourris, and so on, are frequently the most absurd things in the world. First a mysterious introduction; then a terrific bang; a sudden silence; unexpectedly some dance movement; then, to keep up the excitement, by an equally happy thought, a rapid transition to the profound and the pathetic. Thence we are launched into the midst of a tempest; from amid the tempest we pass, after a tantalising pause, to a playful strain, and at the close to a storm of applause, in which everybody embraces everybody with obstreperous ardour. All this finds favour indeed, but why? The truth is simply this—that few have the capacity for giving serious and sustained attention to anything great, even though it were Love itself that wooed them. When a miscellaneous programme is placed before a mixed audience, each person can find something to his taste; and, as he obtains the needful repose during the intervals, he will gladly allow others, during those intervals, to enjoy their favourite pieces. So, if one takes a glance around at operas and concerts, one often finds the ladies noticing the dresses, and the men eyeing the young

On Effect.

Yet effect, in one shape or another, is what attracts the many.

On Effect. ladies, whilst the piece they want is waiting its turn; but the moment that love and dancing come forward, every pleasure-seeking eye is eagerly bent upon the performers. In Milan, where people are not accustomed as in Germany to put much constraint on themselves, and to conceal their natural emotion, it has long been the custom for persons of education to occupy themselves without ceremony with card-playing, but to clap loudly if anything in the music takes their fancy, or at any feat of vocal gymnastics. A great German player, whom I told openly, after a concert, that he had played a bad piece incomparably well, confessed laughingly that his compositions written for the public were not worth a charge of powder.

Sensational Music significant of absence of real power. The prime cause of such unnatural jumbling lies clearly in this, that so very few musicians have the capacity and the gifts necessary to a thorough inspiration by their art. When Handel soars above the clouds, it is the eagle only beginning his heaven-

PURITY IN MUSICAL ART.

ward flight. Many of our fashionable favourites rise with difficulty to the mountain heights, there get giddy, and go back home on foot. Where Handel, unconscious of limitation in his splendid powers, has just made a beginning to an animated chorus, there modern inventiveness usually comes to a stop, and tries to eke itself out by reproducing a former passage perhaps a couple of tones higher, or to supplement its poverty by recitatives, metrical passages, and other make-shifts; whilst, again, where Handel, with a few masterly strokes, closes his passages of grief or bravado, modern mawkishness must whine and bluster on.

But the worst of it is, that under the specious name of effect, the most deadly poison is administered, in the shape of this spasmodic and exaggerated music—this rampant and deafening confusion of sound—stirring up everything ignoble in man, and threatening eventually to annihilate all true sense of music. How can one have patience when it

On Effect.

Debasing tendency of Effect.

On Effect. is announced with much unction that a *Te Deum* is to be performed in a church with an accompaniment of eighty drums; or when, as recently in one of the foremost towns of Germany, the clashing, drumming, and screaming in a opera was so bad that an excellent connoisseur of classical music, on coming out into the street just as forty drummers passed by beating the tattoo, could not help exclaiming, "Thank heaven, we have soft music once more!" If this continues, the result will inevitably be that at our musical repasts we shall never be able to eat our melon without Cayenne pepper, and, like most Russians, must give up brandy and take to aquafortis. There is nothing for it but to put these fuddled musical gluttons and drunkards upon their fast, in order to restore elasticity to their shattered nerves, and to rescue from extinction a pure taste for music as such, and those fine sensibilities, which are ennobled by music, but will not be dragged into and allied with vulgarity and extravagance. In saying this, I would not be supposed to confine my affections wholly to soft plaintive music. Music should portray all states of sensibility, feeling, and passion; but it should treat them poetically; not in their deformity, but in their purity and vigour. Vent your indignation if you please, but do not foam at the mouth; let love burn, as it may, with an all-consuming fire, but not so that the lover, as was recently represented, should, in the very midst of her passionate entreaty, suddenly expire with a light skip. It is incredible what nonsense of this kind the German public have hitherto submitted to. Many of our virtuous maidens, if they knew what they have often to listen to, or themselves to play and sing, and for what purposes one of our most popular composers wrote several pieces with peculiar and masterly skill, would be overwhelmed with shame and indignation. Certain peasants in South Germany are probably the only laymen who hitherto have checked

On Effect.

On Effect.

Effect less objectionable in Oratorio and Opera than in Church music.

abuses, by more than once complaining bitterly to the priest of being obliged by the organist to listen to some low song among his light and trivial pieces.

But, however much the lovers of healthy elevating music may lament its unnatural perversions, they will scarcely effect any appreciable good as regards oratorio and opera, because polite society is in a high state of ferment, because spasmodic and delirious music often harmonises well with poetry and philosophy itself, and also because people regard with favour the claim made, under the pretext of genius, to a certain amount of freedom and license. But, in the case of church music proper, this rage for effect may still be checked; because, as has been already said, the church has nothing to say to the promptings of passion and its accessories. Besides, we may be sure that those who still are warmly attached to the church will gladly hail a worthy style of church music. For the sense of what becomes the

PURITY IN MUSICAL ART.

church is by no means extinct; and it will be found that those preachers who are not content with the poetry of the Psalms of David, but borrow verses from modern poems, or simply give out from the pulpit the name of a modern poet, always create the gravest displeasure.

Unfortunately, however, musicians themselves are almost invariably the obstacle to improvement in this direction. For it often happens that they can only play or write for us music of a profane and trivial character, and laymen who would find fault are bluntly told they know nothing about it. Just as we Germans have a way of at once referring all favourite solecisms to an uniform rule, so our musicians are ever ready with theories to prove black is white; so that it has come to this—that the very works which are the peculiar property of the church are dismissed with a lofty air in the name of so-called science.

Such ill-grounded and unjustifiable mis-

On Effect.

Musicians themselves an obstacle to reform of Church music.

Even acknowledged masterpieces are flouted;

On Effect.

such as the Misereres of Allegri and Bai.

apprehensions on the part of those who are called theorists have now extended to the whole body of old church music; amongst other pieces to the Misereres of Allegri and Bai, which are among the principal performances of Holy Week in the Sistine Chapel, and which have never failed to make the profoundest impression upon listeners; for which reason it was that Mozart made a journey to Rome for the purpose of purloining the music, which had never before been entrusted to any one. The fact that, having been privately communicated to the Emperor Joseph II., they were not appreciated in Vienna, is to be accounted for by both singers and audience being unfavourably predisposed towards them. But that persons professing to have studied music could so superciliously pass by these beautiful pieces, after they had been made known by Burney— at least in their main features, as is evident from other copies—and could positively cast them aside for their want of rhythm, or because their harmony is in the common chord, is one of those incredible things, to be deplored by the lovers of true church music as much as the lately threatened destruction of the chorale itself. I can only express myself upon it in the same language as I have used elsewhere. So once more I say: Is it conceivable that great compositions, based upon a most profound conception, should be thus coldly dismissed—that conception being this, that the satisfaction of a soul, alive to a sense of resignation and blessedness, must lie in what is smooth and unconstrained, again and again recurring to it, and abiding with it. Never yet did any man of fine feeling, who, in solemn reflection gazed on the setting sun, or to whose mind the song of nightingales on a spring evening, or the sighing of the wind in the trees, brought graver thoughts and fancies—never did such an one complain of monotony, and desire, in addition, the embellishment of art. It is precisely in accordance with this great conception that

On Effect.

The conception underlying music of this character explained.

On Effect. those Misereres were composed, in perfect keeping with the prayer, Lord, have mercy on me! uttered in all sincerity and abasement of spirit. There is, therefore, in them no striving after varied effects from love of pretended art, but the burden of the music is developed in constantly recurring passages of Plain-song; and it is the simple beauty of these alternations, with one and the self-same ruling character throughout, which appeals to those devout frames of mind, which are moved, but not agitated. Why is it then that people will not have nowadays more of that which never palls? I possess twenty Cantus Populi in Processione Palmarum by Lasso, from the library of the Conservatoire at Paris, composed in this very style throughout, which, when chastely rendered by a choir in a devotional spirit, cannot fail to produce the most profound impression, entirely written, as they are, in the common chord, evincing in every part the most delicate feeling, and, last not least, always appealing to the same leading idea. *On Effect.*

This same conception may be traced in many hundred pieces of the old church music; and thus there yet remains to the lover of sterling music the consolatory thought that the principles, uniformly observed by so many classical writers in the most vigorous period of composition, must rest upon solid ground; and at any rate are more deserving of attention than the bewildering vagaries whereby people would nowadays fain convey the appearance of genius. *The prevalence of this conception attests its truth and value.*

ON THE USE OF INSTRUMENTS.

On the Use of Instruments.

High estimation of the orchestra in the present day.

I HAVE often seen musicians shrug their shoulders, if a composition has no instrumental score, and I have heard, not less often, a great deal about the necessity of improving such and such orchestral parts, and heard heaven praised that the instrumentation of the present day was what it is, and that the art of it had never been fully understood till now. That this instrumentation has done much for the legitimate objects of serious music, I do not recollect to have heard. On the other hand, in my old friend Luther I read, " Singing is the best art and exercise. It has nothing to do with the world; it is subject to no tribunals or lawsuits. Singers are never troubled, but are glad, and drown their cares in song." So again farther on:

"Music is, as it were, a mistress and a disciplinarian, that makes people softer, gentler, soberer, and more reasonable. Bad fiddlers and violinists serve for our seeing and hearing what a fine art music is; for white is easier seen when in contrast with black." Let us, then, examine the matter somewhat closer, especially with reference to true church music. *On the Use of Instruments.*

No reasonable man will deny that instruments have a great and peculiar advantage, in that they can be much more easily managed than the human voice, have a much larger compass, and, so far, help us to multiply indefinitely the varieties of music. But everything has its time and place, and musicians, as well as others, must conform to this rule. *Advantages of instruments over the voice.*

Our principal churches are lofty and spacious structures, and can only be properly filled by tones possessing roundness, volume, and resonance. Now, this is what is commonly wanting in all but a few wind instru- *Few instruments well adapted for large spaces.*

On the Use of Instruments.

ments, with the notable exception of the trombone, which resembles the human voice in the sonorous tone it gives out, and therefore has always been acceptable in a church. Strings are much too thin for a church, and so are flutes. Twelve good voices would drown fifty such instruments in a church; and

Vocal sound of fine quality injured by instruments.

when voices have a clear, precise, and sustained intonation, the addition of instruments is almost offensive to the ear. Perhaps it was on this account that Pythagoras said that the ring of metal was like the voice of an imprisoned spirit. If we are to indulge in pranks, and, as is now often done, importune the Almighty with drums and fifes, as though we could make merry without Him, then the less said about the laws of art the better. But so far as devotion, humility, and that tempered joy and satisfaction of the inner man which alone befit God's House, are con-

The tongue the real organ of the soul.

cerned, then it should be by the tongue alone, which, after all, is the truest and sincerest exponent of the wants of the soul, that the

PURITY IN MUSICAL ART.

heart's emotions should be outpoured. Grant for a moment that a pianissimo can best be rendered by instruments—a point of which much has been made. But, for the purposes of devotion, we no more want maudlin sentimentality than we do conventional death scenes and starting eyeballs. The Jews' harp, more than any other instrument, dies away, as it were, into nothing; yet I would far rather hear it in a musical box than in a church. It has often been said, and rightly said, that the vocal arts of concert-singers are out of place in a church. On the other hand, I freely confess that the whole Papal choir would be incompetent to take part in a military march, a tattoo, parade-music, or even in that popular song which has lately come out, and which, beginning with muffled drums, passes in the third bar, not to forte nor double forte, but to fortissimo.

An incident occurred not long ago in Paris, very much to the point, which ought to be

On the Use of Instruments. Special instrumental effects not requisite for devotional purposes.

On the Use of Instruments.

Anecdote showing matchless effect of vocal music.

instructive. At Napoleon's coronation the Parisians wished to distinguish themselves by some unprecedented music, and the church was occupied by an orchestra of eighty harps —thus far outdoing King David. Their performance made a great sensation. Immediately afterwards the Pope entered the church, and was received with Scarlatti's mighty "Tu es Petrus," from some thirty singers whom he had brought from Rome, to the utter and instantaneous annihilation of the previous effect. I was told by an eye-witness that the Parisians were so deeply mortified, that they always regarded it as a taunt if any one alluded to the grandeur of their eighty harps.

Presumption against use of instruments in Church music from their omission by the old writers.

Had there been no sufficient reason for excluding instruments from the church, the great old masters, who worked with enthusiasm for the church, would not have failed to avail themselves of them; but, in the main, they do not do so at all. It was not till the vocal music of the Church passed into the oratorio style that accompaniments and interludes were thought of; and then the practice continued to spread—the more so as, eventually, even the operatic style, was impressed into the service of edification. Happily, we have still two churches in which the magnificence of pure vocal music is preserved in its integral purity; the one, the Sistine Chapel; the other, the Imperial Church at St. Petersburg. Both of these have ever been, and are at the present moment, the admiration alike of those who understand music and those who do not, by reason of the music there performed; and only quite lately a German musician, who had returned from Rome, and had no leanings to the Roman Church, but was much opposed to it, told me that he had for the first time discovered what the perfection of devotional music was, from the singing in the Sistine Chapel.

I do not for a moment deny the peculiar charm of instruments for certain purposes. I do not deny, for instance, that gracefulness

On the Use of Instruments.

Purely vocal music still preserved at Rome and St. Petersburg.

Instruments invaluable for certain purposes:

On the Use of Instruments.

and rapidity; that romping, bustle, and tumult, and dancing, may be a far fitter subject—a thousand times fitter if you will—for instruments than for the voice. But let us put all things in the places for which they are fitted. Bright red and bright yellow are very beautiful colours; yet we should not endure a figure of Christ draped in a bright yellow mantle, and a bright rose-coloured girdle.

but their associations essentially secular.

Any one who, with devout purpose of mind, listens in church to well-known instrumental pieces, will always find, that as soon as ever the instruments become busy, the world enters into his thoughts. I know that this is what many people like. But why? For no other reason than that they are only too glad to be reminded in church of the things which please them outside it.

Instances of extreme abuse in this respect.

But the most unendurable thing is, that instruments have of late been employed to mark a climax, suggestive of orgies in a church; that an Amen, or an Hallelujah, or a Gloria in Excelsis Deo, has been accompanied by the thunder of drums and the crash of trumpets; and even that resort has not unfrequently been had to guns and cannon discharged in the vicinity of the church. Is it possible so utterly to forget what we are, and what we ought to be? When we praise God in church, there should be no room for any other thought but that we are standing before God's throne. But is it possible to imagine a congregation entering Heaven with songs of praise, and introducing first timbrels and trumpets, and behind them a train of artillery, and then, as they draw near to God's throne, rushing forward with profane plaudits? Singular is it, indeed, how prone we are to overlook the good we possess, and to pursue something wrong. For we have within the church itself, in the collective voice of the congregation, the simplest and grandest of all means for attaining a climax worthy of divine worship. Let Hallelujah, Amen, be sung by the choir from the organ-loft or chancel; and then, if the whole congregation simply recite

On the Use of Instruments.

Showing utter forgetfulness of the nature of worship.

Amazing effect of the congregational voice.

the words after them, one might imagine oneself transported into Heaven, or, further, realise to oneself that such is the manner after which God is worshipped in Heaven. St. Chrysostom, in his exposition of the 41st Psalm, has said, and said very well, much that bears upon this point. But he goes on to speak of a purified mind, and of mortification of the flesh; and so, alas! of qualities to which our restless dazed amateurs are strangers. For which reason it is not easy to say to them, as Chrysostom did to his well-disciplined singers, "When you take your place in God's choir, you may count yourselves as at David's side. There no zithers or strings are required."

It must, however, be confessed that, with our present choirs, but little can be achieved. In utter disregard of the example and precepts of Gregory the Great in the Roman, and of Luther in the Protestant Church, hardly anything has been done of late in Germany for a supply of good voices; and

Marginalia:
On the Use of Instruments.
St. Chrysostom's view of the singers' office.
Choirs neglected.

even the choristers whom we could have controlled have been allowed to disperse, partly, as I know for a fact, because the music is said to interfere with the sermon, though it must be evident that sermons of real merit can only gain by hearts being prompted to devotion by fine and truly spiritual music.

On the Use of Instruments.

We must, however, consider the subject of instrumentation, without reference to time or place, more distinctly.

Instrumentation in general.

It seems to have become a favourite idea to keep all the instruments constantly employed. That a timid composer, who cannot face the frowns of players obliged to be temporarily silent, should be governed by this idea, is quite natural; and this probably is the origin of a French opera, which has been given in Germany times innumerable within the last ten years, in the overture to which all singing birds strike up on all sides. But though even a lover of art can, in a pleasure hour, heartily enjoy this kind of thing, inasmuch as its sheer absurdity renders it harm-

Too constant use of the whole orchestra.

On the Use of Instruments.

Each instrument has its proper character.

Illustration: Handel's Dead March.

less, yet it is necessary to protest most seriously against its becoming the rule.

As, with the human voice, each variety has its own qualities—ponderous passages being, for instance, suitable for a bass; elegant, tender, and fanciful ones for a tenor or soprano; and melancholy, pathetic ones for a contralto; so, too, each instrument has its own domain. The trombone may perchance sound in Heaven, but upon earth never to a soft amorous air; and the delicate flute must be silent when a weightier wind-instrument utters its graver note, and may fitly be associated with the viola. As an example, I would adduce Handel's famous Dead March in Saul—the work of a composer who worked with the might of a Jupiter, gave with unerring instinct to each voice the music that suited it, who knew and frequently employed all the principal instruments of the present day, and who, therefore, it may fairly be inferred, had his own good reasons whenever he omitted to employ one of the usual instruments. In this march the flutes in the earlier bars are altogether silent; then they make themselves heard; presently they break off, but soon after again enter and predominate to the end. The reason is obvious—that Handel, great and healthful spirit that he was, treats deep sorrow with respect, but does not leave us in unmanly despondency; and therefore, as a friend who consoles and sustains, he laments with those that lament, but at last lets in the sun; and hence it is that, after hearing one of his mourning choruses, we often feel more composed and serene than after the most cheerful effusions of modern sentimentalism. Thus, the March begins with utter prostration in grief, which the subsequent entry of the flutes seeks to alleviate; and after a relapse, which again is entirely in accordance with nature, the flutes attend the mourners to the close. All this is as clear as day. Nevertheless, I have heard a performance of this March, specially designed for effect, in which the flutes

On the Use of Instruments.

On the Use of Instruments.

were from the commencement brought into necessary collision with the weightier wind instruments, and by sheer sweetness spoilt the whole character of the piece. With regard to this, however, it might be said that Handel's masterpieces are incapable of being utterly ruined; and, accordingly, on the occasion in question, the audience were pretty well satisfied.

Modern accompaniments not always creditable.

If it be true that modern instrumentation deserves especial praise, it should be shown that the furnishing of suitable accompaniments has been undertaken with diligence and success. But the evidence on this point is extremely doubtful. The whole manner in which rocking, rolling, skipping, noisy accompaniments are associated with the most pensive and gentle airs, shows clearly enough the utter absence of taste. The accompaniment to a song is often positively distressing; what would be effective under other circumstances being often clumsily introduced in the wrong place. Take for instance a Con-

PURITY IN MUSICAL ART.

tinuo, as it is called, where the bass goes its own way with a decided and rapid movement, under certain circumstances with really fine effect; its tendency in an imposing passage being to inspire the singers, and urge them ever higher and higher. It is in this way that B. Durante has used it in his "Magnificat," Caldara in a "Lauda Sion Salvatorem," and Handel in the Chorus "But the waters." Tempted by the device, a modern composer has in an oratorio given us a continuo by way of support to a supplicatory duet for two tenors, which travels along like a storm wind, and can only be appreciated when the voice parts are omitted. Even Mozart, in spite of his marvellously fine taste, has, in this matter of accompaniments, forgotten himself, as only his blind admirers can fail to see. This is signally the case in his edition of the Messiah, where, more than anywhere else, he should have observed the greatest caution. Every page of it shows such overloading and interpolating as would unquestionably have been

On the Use of Instruments.

Mozart has sinned in this respect in his additions to the "Messiah."

On the Use of Instruments. repudiated as misplaced by the great author of that immortal work. I shall only mention, by way of example, the fine bass air, "The people that walked in darkness." This incomparable piece is throughout serious in character, and requires corresponding repose in the accompaniment. Here, therefore, Handel employs violins and basses only, which, with him, assuredly does not mean, as appears to be supposed, a couple of thin violins, and a single bass player, but just as much effective support as the vocalist can bear—a hundred instruments if you like, supposing he has the throat of a giant. But Mozart has unadvisedly called in the aid of flutes, clarionets, and bassoons. They enter at the fourth bar, as if some one had to be wakened up, cease directly afterwards, but, with an unhappy tendency to tone-painting, come in again at the words "A great light;" again are silent, presently return, and so on. It may be said that this treatment is but a fresh illustration of Mozart's genius, but in this passage he has murdered Handel, and taken away the whole character of the solo. The heart-stirring bass air, "For this mortal," has suffered a similar fate in Schwenck's pianoforte arrangement. Mozart had unaccountably omitted it; Schwenck re-annexed it, but with a peculiar and agitated accompaniment, which may tax the dexterity of a good player, but is incompatible with the profound intention of the piece. *[On the Use of Instruments.]*

The modern practice of filling up has, indeed, been alleged to be necessary in the case of Handel's oratorio scores, on the ground that he supplemented them so fully by his masterly organ-play. Then why do we not aim at that same masterly rendering, those very same conditions which originally gave to his oratorios their perfect fulness and dignity? And is it to be supposed that Handel, in this organ-play, showed himself off, and spoilt his own work? This I do believe—that at those passages where, in the *[Handel's Oratorios should be represented as intended by him.]*

On the Use of Instruments.

vocal score, we find the brief direction "full organ," the almightiness of sound was to be heard when Handel played the organ,—such a volume of sound as a thousand fiddlers or flutists could not now reproduce. And, indeed, to sum the matter up, who would ever dream of tricking out a Homer, a Dante, or a Shakspeare in a modern dress?

A bad band the worst accompaniment.

Lastly, I must say this to all those who love truth. If it be insisted upon that no good can come without an instrumental accompaniment, let us at all events have something better offered to us than is usually the case. Let us have, I would say, not a row of players half of whom are like stocks, incapable of grasping the spirit of a work, paying no attention to the voices, caring only to make their own instruments heard, and regardless of the quality of the tones they produce. Better have but three choristers in a church than charlatans who bring shame upon music. Whilst, for this reason, I verily believe that Handel's oratorios, if not given in a church, nor again in a theatre, but in a good hall, with a not too numerous body of singers, and with an efficient pianoforte accompaniment, would come out far more impressively than if supported by a bad orchestra; at the same time I am free to confess that a clear and full instrumental accompaniment, such as was employed under Handel's own direction, must enhance twofold the splendour of his oratorios. But in speaking of a pianoforte accompaniment, I am supposing that the player is no blunderer, that he does not strum through his part, or lose sight of the voices, or try to create a sensation by rapid fingering, but has, on the contrary, so to speak, all the voices in his ten fingers, supports them wherever they falter, and occupies his right hand with the full tones of the middle octaves as much as possible, always endeavouring, by giving the chords fully, to make it readily felt to what key a particular passage belongs. For this last reason I much dislike the pianoforte

On the Use of Instruments.

An intelligent pianoforte accompaniment to Handel's Oratorios preferable to a bad orchestra.

On the Use of Instruments.

arrangements which have come into such favour. For the high notes which sound full and melodious with strings and wind instruments, become in the same octave on the keys a miserable jingle: besides which these arrangements prevent a close attention to the full score, without which no good can be achieved. Had Handel foreseen the possibility of his Messiah being rendered without full organ and instrumental accompaniment, and merely with the pianoforte, and had he himself written a special accompaniment for this purpose, it would certainly have been something quite different from Schwenck's overburdened arrangement, much as we may recognise his exemplary fidelity.

Overpowering of voices by Instruments.

However highly we may value and extol the orchestra, we must never go so far as to connive at the offence, so common of late, of utterly disregarding the voices in church music, and allowing an extravagant and meddlesome predominance to the instrumental accompaniment. I shall not now instance living German composers, for that might be considered personal. I shall only mention a foreigner of the present day, and of much genius, whom my thoughts are not likely to reach — Cherubini. Examine his sacred publications, and a little reflection will at once show that his orchestral accompaniments conflict with his vocal parts. Yet his great name as an opera-writer has hitherto blinded his undiscerning admirers to his shortcomings in church music; although he himself would hardly set much value on those works, and would much more likely complain of having been the victim of the miserable Parisian taste. For he is the very man who promoted the recent publication of old Italian works, and especially of Marcello's great Psalm-book; and I am assured that he always has Palestrina by his side. Moreover, following the example of the great old masters, he has set the Creed for eight voices, filling a whole folio, and containing some

On the Use of Instruments.

Cherubini an offender in this respect.

On the Use of Instruments. incomparable pieces, but never handed to the printer, because the gay Parisian world did not appreciate it, and was not worthy of it: and the whole of this fine work is laid out for voices only.

ON A CAREFUL JUDGING OF GREAT MASTERS' WORKS.

On a careful judging of Great Masters' Works.

IT is undeniable that in one way an immense deal is being done for music in Germany at the present time—infinitely more than in Italy, the land of so many immortal composers. In other words, we are labouring with burning zeal to acquire execution, and those who are thorough adepts in crossing the hands and intertwining the fingers, even sacrifice bodily and mental health to compass impossibilities. Thus it is that those who have attained a certain amount of execution are often very irritable and capricious, passionately extolling the merits of their favourite pieces, but wholly incompetent to form an intelligent judgment upon a composition's intrinsic worth. Such is

Execution now the chief object of study.

On a careful judging of Great Masters' Works.

As such it is merely lost labour,

ever the case when the essence of a thing is lost sight of; and yet how easily might the right path be found!

In music it can be of no concern to us to stand gaping at a player's fingers, or to see trashy pieces wonderfully elaborated; but it is the ear that ought to be charmed, without regard to what mechanical difficulties may be in the way. It is, perhaps, excusable in peripatetic performers to play the surest game in their tours, and to show the outside of which they are capable and nothing less, because the public would, as a rule, sooner see a rope-dancer stand on his head than that he should attempt to set before them patterns of form by graceful and easy movements. But it grieves one to the heart that on all sides time, money, and health should be flung away for the sake of acquiring what is without value or meaning; and that, from a constant straining after startling effects, the art of rendering simple pieces with passion, tenderness, and good phrasing, should almost utterly perish. The music now in vogue possesses no kind of moral influence whatever, unless it be the encouragement of vanity, and of addiction to dancing and pleasure. There is only this consolation, that when the years of childishness and pleasure-seeking are passed, these *tours-de-force* are usually given up, and those who were so fortunate as to learn in their youth soothing, delightsome, and elevating melodies, retain for them, even in extreme old age, the liveliest interest. The present condition of things may enable us to understand the lamentations of Greek authors over the injurious effects of their later music; and well might one wish to return to the schools of which Aristophanes tells us in the "Clouds," that the boys there were taught to sing the songs of their forefathers slowly and soberly, and that they got some sharp raps if they attempted to embellish them by flourishes.

The mistake of overdoing things is cer-

On a careful judging of Great Masters' Works. and without any moral influence for good.

On a careful judging of Great Masters' Works.

Modern straining of instrumental and vocal compass.

tainly far more prevalent in our time than it was in that of our forefathers. For our instruments are much more various, and each one has properties pertaining to itself, and not to others. Yet nothing is considered to be beyond an instrument's reach, and players seem fondest of being heard when their instruments outstep their respective provinces, or show their weakest points. The Jew's harp and French horn must needs execute light runs, like a violin; the violin copies the poverty of the pianoforte; the trumpet must be tender like the flute; and the venerable cumbrous double-bass has lately tried to imitate the graceful turns of every sort of instrument. The audacity of excess has even invaded the domain of the voice, and evidently many composers care not a rush where mortal basses, tenors, altos, and sopranos have their bounds. It is certain, for instance, that the alto proper, which sings down to  cannot well rise above . And yet E flat, E natural, and F, and even more, are frequently required from them, even by C. P. E. Bach, in his "Holy, Holy, Holy," though in such a way as to admit of remedy, as he does not take the altos below 𝄞, so that the alto part can be taken by the second soprani. Even choir-masters, who were all for the modern style, have more than once expressed to me their regret at such liberties. But whence the abuse? Our great old writers have never countenanced it in their works. How well suited to each voice is Handel's score; and how careful in this matter were even the most animated Italian masters, such as Caldara, Marcello, and Durante, although as a rule Italian voices are higher, deeper, and clearer than German! Durante studied moderation of this kind, even when he wrote for practice, and sought, like a very Mephistophiles, to lay all sorts of traps for his female singers—*e.g.* in his twelve duets for soprano and alto,

On a careful judging of Great Masters' Works.

On a careful judging of Great Masters' Works.

Confusion of means and ends in this respect.

in his eighteen duets for solfaing for soprano and bass, in his "Lezione del Venerdi Santo," for soprano, and in his Seven Cantate Morali for contralto. As then our composers cannot plead, like Hasse, that their Faustinas can reach anything, and as they write for those whose name is legion, such extremes must be utterly condemned, howsoever they may be explained. For pedantry is one of our marked characteristics, and leads us to confound means and ends. Thus, what is properly only a part of training must needs be exhibited in public, and hence naturally arises the evil in question. Any one who wants to sing a high note perfectly should be able to sing some notes yet higher. These extreme notes must indeed be practised, but, thereafter, they have no proper place in a performance that must be faultless; just as the Paris dancing-masters put leaden soles on the children's feet some hours before they dance, and then, when the time comes, take off the weight, and thus

PURITY IN MUSICAL ART.

obtain the most perfect facility for the result. But our musicians are only too ready to let their leaden soles remain on as parts of the costume; and so bravura practice-pieces, which might have qualified a person to render works of simpler character and of real feeling, come, in general, to usurp their place.

On a careful judging of Great Masters' Works.

Meanwhile, the true basis of musical knowledge—simple thorough-bass—is, in spite of all good theoretical treatises, often most unjustifiably neglected, not merely by amateurs, but even by music-masters, precentors, and organists, though it admits of no doubt that a fine sense of harmony can only be properly formed by thorough-bass, and even that perfect facility and certainty of execution is impossible without it. Unhappily, our musicians, engrossed in their artificial lucubrations, generally lose sight of the essence of music, fail to perceive the dignity of their art, and think by display to establish a pretension to talent.

Neglect of thorough-bass.

This display is in every craft the bane of

On a careful judging of Great Masters' Works.

To judge of a composer rightly the scrutiny must be thorough and complete.

Inequality a trait of the greatest genius.

our times. For it diverts us from labour; and without labour, trouble, and care, nothing can legitimately prosper. To get at the real essence of music, a man must study full scores closely; must, with vocal pieces, sing them through himself, passing from one part to another, so as to see exactly where lies the gist of the music; and he must endeavour to familiarise himself with the great masters in their entirety. For it is just the characteristic of the greatest geniuses that they do not, like middling composers, maintain an uniform level, but flag at times, when the spirit needs to recover from a great creative effort. Hume says somewhere that Frenchmen are like cucumbers, a nice fruit, but like the one to the other: Englishmen are like melons; five out of ten may be thrown aside as fit for nothing, but the rest taste all the more delicious. And so it often is with the works of really great composers, and young musicians will be led astray if they form their judgment from this or that piece, without taking trouble to acquaint themselves with their author in his entirety. I regard Palestrina as a very angel among composers; yet I possess six of his masses in which I find nothing of special note, while I consider his Missa Papæ Marcelli a colossal work of art, and many of his other works as altogether unique and unsurpassed. The same may be said of Caldara, Lotti, Durante, and many others—even of Handel himself; for he composed rapidly, was often compelled to work, often mentally harassed, and for some years suffered from gout; so that his operas and oratorios (of course with some exceptions) may be likened to boxes containing jewels wrapped in cotton wool; and I can only pity those who impose upon themselves the unconditional duty of giving an oratorio of Handel's in its entirety, as if they were thereby achieving something wonderful.

It is notorious that our performers, composers, and music-masters, are, as a rule, utterly ignorant of all works more than fifty

On a careful judging of Great Masters' Works.

E.g. with Palestrina and Handel.

Unaccountable ignorance of old composers.

On a careful judging of Great Masters' Works.

years old. Whilst in all other pursuits—in poetry, in painting, in architecture, and the rest, we labour diligently to bring to light the collective productions of a great Past, to make them clear, and to bring them back to life; the masterpieces of the greatest musical composers are meantime doomed to remain buried, and, one might even say, a laughing-stock to shallow ignorant babblers. Our musicians are not even influenced by any worldly curiosity and ambition. Luther,—man of loftiest, healthiest spirit,—was devoted, heart and soul, to music. His great favourite was Senffel. There is an old story of him that one evening, after having had a motett of Senffel's sung, he exclaimed in ecstasy, "If I were to die for it, I could not write a motett like that;" and yet antiquarians of Lutheran sympathies take not the slightest trouble to obtain a notion of the manner and method of this great musician. Yet more unpardonable is it that, excepting some attempts in Munich, absolutely nothing has

Of Senffel, for instance;

been done for Orlando di Lasso, the change of whose name from the Flemish Roland Lass into the soft Italian form, has not despoiled him of German vigour. For in his day (he was born 1520, and died in 1594) he was accounted, not only in Germany, but in other countries, as almost one of the wonders of the world. Summoned to Munich, he presided there over a choir, the like of which Germany never saw before, and is scarcely likely to see again. Most of his numerous compositions were printed, disseminated all over Europe, and everywhere highly esteemed. By favour of a member of the Pope's choir, I have in my possession a mass of his for four voices, upon the title-page of which the old Roman copyists have written "Hic est Lassus, qui lassum recreat orbem:" (this is the Lassus (*i.e.* the weary one), who refreshes the weary world.) Charles IX., in order to obtain repose for his soul after the massacre of St. Bartholomew, commissioned him to set the Penitential Psalms to music.

On a careful judging of Great Masters' Works.

of Orlando di Lasso;

On a careful judging of Great Masters' Works.

This colossal work still exists in the Library at Munich, adorned with gold and jewels, and portraits of the composers of that date. But where, I should like to know, is the young musician who has ever travelled thither to study this and other works of this incomparable master there to be found? I might add that the authorities of St. Mark at Venice could easily write upon their little fingernails the names of the German virtuosi who, within the last thirty years, have inquired *of Lotti;* there for the works of Lotti.

and of Handel. But what is unpardonable upon any consideration is the general neglect of Handel, whose works may be collected without much trouble in English editions in full score, and in correct and very readable type, forming an inestimable treasury of the most genuine and masterly music of nearly every style. Handel was the Shakspeare of music, and well deserved to be laid near the great poet in Westminster Abbey. At home in every species of musical contrivance, to a degree

PURITY IN MUSICAL ART.

rarely seen, he stands out in all kinds of musical form as an immortal pattern for imitation, fresh, animated, and adroit, as though all were sport to him. In all styles, from the fond and playful to the sublime, he has furnished us with incomparable specimens of inspiration and refinement. In the staid music of the great church style alone has he done but little, because his communion and his entourage were not such as to impel him thereto; but of his genius and knowledge in that branch there can be no question, as is proved (to go no farther) by the first chorus in "Susanna," and the chorus, "The earth swallowed them," in "Israel."

In Germany, we usually hear mentioned first the Messiah, next, perhaps, Judas Maccabæus, Samson, Alexander's Feast, and, quite recently, now that there are arrangements for the piano for the benefit of the unskilled, certain other pieces; but nothing is more certain than that Handel's works, if we refuse to single out for animadversion

On a careful judging of Great Masters' Works.

Versatility of his genius.

On a careful judging of Great Masters' Works.

His Oratorios.

some particular portion that is defective or indifferent, deserve to be described as a very ocean-world of splendour. I shall make no reference to his pianoforte works, nor to his more important instrumental works, which together fill more than eighty folios; nor to his forty or fifty operas, some of which were received, even in Italy, with rapture; but only to those works which were most congenial to his lofty spirit when circumstances allowed it free play—I mean to his oratorios in the broadest sense. His chamber-duets and cantatas, written as early as between 1710 and 1721, his Grand Jubilate (Hundredth Psalm), the Dettingen Te Deum, the Utrecht Te Deum, and the twelve Anthems written for the Duke of Chandos, disclose the giant strength and the rare qualities of this mighty artist. After the production of these works, circumstances caused him to turn his attention almost entirely to the theatre. But after the appearance of Esther in 1731, his genius became more and more addicted to high enterprise ; and now there appear, prior to the "Messiah," and containing, without exception, incomparable numbers, Deborah, Athalia, Acis and Galatea, Alexander's Feast, Ode to St. Cecilia, Israel in Egypt (a work of infinite grandeur), the Allegro and Penseroso, Saul, and other short pieces of similar calibre. In 1741 and 1742 follow the marvellous and transcendent Messiah and Samson. Yet is the solid strength of the master in no way reduced by all this, but only set in motion. For there follow now in rapid succession, and studded with brilliant gems, Semele, Belshazzar, Susanna, Hercules, Choice of Hercules, Time and Truth, the Occasional, Joseph, Judas Maccabæus, Joshua, Alexander Balus, Solomon, Theodora, and, lastly, the oratorio of Jephtha, written with such freshness and animation, as though his advancing years were still inspired with the full vigour of youth and manhood. Hence I yield, upon the whole, a hearty assent to all that the English

On a careful judging of Great Masters' Works.

On a careful judging of Great Masters' Works.

Busby's estimate of Handel.

writer Busby has recently said about Handel in his History of Music, to the following effect:—" As a man, Handel may justly be ranked among the moral and the pious; as a scholar, with the general class of the well-educated; but, as a musician, he is above all rank, for no one ranks with him. His ideas had never any alliance with tameness or inanity; his invention appears to have been always ready, rich, and wonderfully accommodating to the subject in hand, whether gay or serious, cheerful or solemn, light or grand. He wrote quickly; but the motion of his pen could rarely keep pace with the rapidity of his imagination, and most of his finest thoughts were the birth of a moment. For the most part, he is very original; and, where he shines the brightest, the lustre is uniformly his own; yet whatever he appropriates, he improves. It has been said of him, as of Cicero, that whatever he touched he turned to gold; but it might with more correctness be affirmed that his judgment rejected what was not ori-

PURITY IN MUSICAL ART.

ginally gold, and that the gold he borrowed he refined. In some composers we find sweetness, in others grace; in these tenderness, in those dignity; here we feel the sentiment and force of character proper to the theatre, there are struck with the grandeur and the solemnity claimed by the service of the church; but in Handel we discover all these properties; and what indisputably entitles him to pre-eminence over all other musicians, ancient and modern, is the truth, that, while he equals all others in every style but one, in that one he transcends them all: his mellifluous softness and dignified mirth, fire, energy, and purity of pathos, have been approached by various masters; but to his sublimity no one has been able to soar. While I listen to his 'Hallelujah' Chorus in the 'Messiah,' his 'Horse and his Rider' in 'Israel in Egypt,' or the nobler portions of his Dettingen Te Deum, the massy grandeur appeals not only to my ear but to my soul; it seems even to excite another sense; I

On a careful judging of Great Masters' Works.

see the glory that is celebrated, and am profane enough to extend its image to the composer."

Anybody who knows the principal works of Lasso, Palestrina, Lotti, and Sebastian Bach, must certainly pronounce this last dictum, so far as it excludes all other composers, an exaggeration; but an exaggeration may easily be forgiven where the object of eulogy is not over-estimated in itself, and when it proceeds from so just an appreciation of the great and true.

In conclusion, I take leave to address to my fellow-countrymen a few remarks on the arrangements of Handel's Oratorios.

In these arrangements one of two objects must be in view; either to have selected pieces for those who cannot compass entire works (and this must, as a rule, be the case with all choral societies); or else to have a faithful reproduction of the original work as composed by its author. To take a middle course by a process of dismemberment and

On a careful judging of Great Masters' Works.

Unjustifiable treatment of Handel at the hands of Editors.

re-arrangement, is a piece of barefaced presumption, which may perhaps be pardoned for once in a Mozart, but in no one else. Who is there that may stand near Handel, or should I not say, above Handel? and why should we disguise the original text, and forestal the free judgment of those who do not share our taste? These musical transmogrifications are as reprehensible as Wieland's arbitrary version of Shakspeare; and it is to be hoped, for the honour of musicians, that such abuses will no longer find apologists. I know, indeed, that my countrymen will dare everything. But it is time to have done with these perversions, for we have had enough of them. To begin with, Mozart treated the "Messiah" with the utmost freedom, not merely re-scoring it, but likewise leaving out several airs, an entire chorus, and one of the finest recitatives, and also transposing for a bass a whole piece which Handel had divided between bass and soprano. So, again, in the editions of the Hundredth

On a careful judging of Great Masters' Works.

As in the "Messiah;"

On a careful judging of Great Masters' Works.

and in "Samson."

Psalm, the fine alto lead has been excised with unsparing hand. Lastly, in the edition of Samson, published by Marchetti in Vienna, Mosel has crowned the career of license. It was, indeed, hard to believe that this editor would have permitted himself the smallest alteration of such a work. For Handel himself doubted whether he ought not to place Samson above even the "Messiah;" so that it should have been the first obligation to eschew the slightest falsification of the text. Yet, what do we find in this edition? First-rate choruses are omitted; the most beautiful airs, duets, and recitatives are omitted; a weak translation is appended, one of the finest bass pieces is reconstructed, in order to join on with the one that follows, intervening portions having been expunged; and in the second chorus an interpolated Presto has been foisted into the 31st bar, for which there is neither rhyme nor reason. Consequently, one can only connect this Samson with the hero himself, by conceiving of him with his eyes put out and his hair cut off!

If, then, selections are given, they may be determined according to your taste, after previous consultation with competent musicians; but be sure to choose the very best specimens from the entire range of Handel's works. They will form an ample supply for years for a vocal society that has only one evening free in a week. But if the wants of connoisseurs are to be studied, give everything, without exception, in its original form; especially as all persons have moments of inattention, and fail to catch on one day what they will appreciate the next. This is particularly applicable to works of real genius, for their authors do not usually write to an uniform standard. Moreover, knowledge of a master's whole nature,—his faults, therefore, as well as his virtues,—is an indispensable condition to a well-grounded estimate of him. Shakspeare and Cervantes contain paradoxes, like Durante or Handel; but no

On a careful judging of Great Masters' Works.

Selections good for particular purposes, but insufficient for real knowledge.

On a careful judging of Great Masters' Works.

man of intelligence would wish them away, inasmuch as they afford matter for reflection, and because the mere petulance of genius may well indicate its commanding power.

ON A LIBERAL JUDGMENT.

A THOROUGH study of individual authors is indispensable: yet it may prove highly dangerous; for men seldom possess comprehensiveness of judgment, indefatigability, and largeness of mind. Hence, they are far too eager to be great in a confined sphere, and affect a vast importance for their own narrow views.

And this is a mischief that obtains, unfortunately, to a large extent in music. Handelians decline acquaintance with Mozart; the admirers of Mozart do likewise by Handel; followers of Bach ignore Marcello; and thus the foibles of each favourite come to be regarded as paragons; blind admiration being less troublesome than thoughtful criticism. Even style is not beyond the reach of this

On a liberal judgment.

Evil of addiction to particular authors,

On a liberal judgment, and particular styles.

folly. It would be every bit as sensible to dispute on the respective beauties of crimson and purple, or blue and green, as upon the question, whether a love-song is more beautiful than a bravado one, or a soft plaintive air than a wild and vehement one. Nevertheless, it always happens after a miscellaneous performance, that, instead of thanking God for providing them with all the forms of beauty, good folk worry themselves to death as to which piece, after all, when maturely considered, and minutely examined, and probed to its depths, is strictly the best; and then, perhaps, are much injured if others see no point in their doggedness.

It is impossible to utter too emphatic a warning against such miserable narrowness. Why, when we find ourselves in a country abounding in flowers of all kinds, should we be transfixed by the beauty of only one, and, instead of studying variety in our nosegay, pass over all others for the sake of one? or why, at a well-furnished table, should we refuse all sorts of good things out of preference for one favourite dish? We deprive ourselves of the highest enjoyment in music, if we aim at extinguishing every composer and every style but one. For, as a rule, every composer has his own particular charm; and herein lies the infinite power of perfect music, that it can stir, purify, and ennoble the heart and soul of man in all kinds of ways. Graun (and likewise Rolle and Homilius) had not Handel's genius; but the devotional and childlike spirit of his "Death of Jesus" will and must render it immortal, like Handel's "Messiah." So, again, Glück certainly had not that exquisite refinement, and that delicate and ethereal fragrance that distinguishes Mozart; but who would assert that Mozart's writings were pervaded by the same fresh and vigorous instinct of romance and grandeur that are so conspicuous in every line of Glück's great works? I have already expressed in more than one place my unbounded admiration of

On a liberal judgment.

Different composers have different points of excellence.

On a liberal judgment.

Palestrina; yet I affirm that he could never have written Mozart's "Don Juan," any more than Homer could have written Hamlet; while I also affirm, on the other hand, that Mozart could not have written the "Missa Papæ Marcelli," the "Song of Solomon," the eight-part Magnificat, and the Responsoria of Palestrina. The question what Mozart might have produced under different circumstances is one I of course cannot answer; and it must be understood that I only speak of the prevailing tendency of his genius as continually evidenced by his works—precisely the same ground upon which rests my estimate of Palestrina. Occasionally the most superb passages occur side by side with egregious failures. The tawdry poverty of Marcello's Cantatas, and his great collection of Psalms, is quite terrible; yet, where is a bolder composer than he, and where the music that reveals the spirit of the profound and stately Greek modes so well as Marcello's? We may be sure that his countrymen, who upon an average have a better musical instinct than the Germans, had good ground for calling him the Pindar of their musicians. *On a liberal judgment.*

There is yet another mischievous habit to encounter in our assault upon one-sidedness, and that is national and even local exclusiveness, which has ever stood in the way, not of adopting a bad style and manner from foreign countries, but of fairly estimating their chief works. Of late years, now that everything German has become an object of native worship—for the most part, I admit, with the best intentions, but seldom with discrimination and reflection—this evil has greatly increased; and there are certain estimable young men of my acquaintance who will not hear of any but German pictures and compositions. *German exclusiveness.*

Such well-meant ungraciousness may be all very well where arms are concerned; but in the case of the arts and sciences, and, above all, in the case of music, it is folly. *Folly of depreciating Italian music.*

On a liberal judgment.

German music has many splendid and incomparable works to show, of the very first order of beauty; but Italian music is also for its part so infinitely rich, of such characteristic genius, so completely the reflex of the ever-blue Italian sky which lends to all their works an almost unearthly charm, that to cast aside their masterpieces, and, as it were, to refuse a journey to Naples and Sicily, because of our own beautiful pine forests, can only be called the most downright national pedantry. Have we, indeed, come to this, that, to be consistent, every one, according to his birthplace, is to have his own particular favourite in music; and, according as he may have been born in Vienna or Berlin, to ignore Sebastian Bach, Handel, Hasse, and Graun, on the one hand, and Glück, Haydn, Mozart, and Beethoven on the other?

Imputation of effeminacy to Italian music misplaced.

We often, indeed, hear ignorant and foolish talk of German music being masculine and robust, Italian simply effeminate. But what if it were so? We always thank Heaven for providing Adam with an amiable wife; and should we not laugh, if it were gravely asked whether a perfectly beautiful and refined youth were a higher prize than a perfectly beautiful and refined maiden? But the imputation rests upon a pure figment. True it is that Italian music often has much more softness, delicacy, grace, and angelic purity than German; but there are Italian authors who do not yield in vigour to the Germans. Durante is often far softer than Handel; yet we may confidently place his "Dixit Dominus" beside Handel's Hundredth Psalm. Nor would Handel, again, have allowed for an instant that Alessandro Scarlatti was an effeminate composer. On the contrary, in that very Hundredth Psalm, he has borrowed from that great master; just as Graun, in his "Death of Jesus," has borrowed from several · of Durante's works, hitherto unknown in Germany.

Let us then, as our own great composers did in times past, apply ourselves with a will

On a liberal judgment.

On a liberal judgment. All jealousy to be put aside.

to learn from Italians not only music, but impartiality. Handel was well-nigh worshipped in Italy, and one of his operas had to be repeated in Florence twenty-seven consecutive times. Hasse obtained in Rome, and retains to this day, the appellation of "the divine Saxon," and was in many respects imitated by Italians. How they have never ceased to honour Mozart is well known. So let us, on our part, set aside all egotism, and repeat with Hasse "the divine Lotti," and with Sebastian Bach "the glorious Caldara."

ON MISADAPTATIONS OF TEXT.

On Misadaptations of Text.

To the mistaken ideas of music in the present day is mainly due the growing evil of texts altogether wanting in taste, and not unfrequently devoid of meaning. Music has no better ally than well-chosen words. An appropriate text directs the soul to the object which it is the office of music still further to enhance; and to choose a bad text would be as great a folly as to adorn a maiden's head with a dish in lieu of a wreath. Is it not from the text that Cherubini's delightful Water-carrier derives a portion of his charm? and are not the sublime words of Handel's "Messiah" quite incomparable as a support and enhancement of the music? And in Zumsteg's most successful work "Colma," it is certain that the declamatory

Alliance of words and music.

PURITY IN MUSICAL ART.

On Misadaptations of Text.

merit of the text had a marked influence upon the music.

Of the opera I have nothing farther to say. It is no better than a feather in the eddy of a whirlwind; and all we can do is to wonder when it will abate its extravagance. Serious music, however, is not so dependent on the vagaries of unenlightened fashion; and there is the more hope of its improvement, as the taste for ancient poetry, and so for simplicity and vigour, is on the increase.

It must be owned that our esteemed countryman Klopstock has set a bad example in the way of text-mutilation. We have no grander, I might say, no more stupendous church hymn than the Stabat Mater. Every word of it is as weighty as fine gold. Klopstock adapted the German text to Pergolesi's music; but how did he do it? The opening words, "Stabat Mater dolorosa juxta crucem lacrimosa, dum pendebat Filius," are thus rendered: "Jesus Christ hung on the Cross, downwards sank

Mutilation of the hymn "Stabat Mater."

His bleeding head, bleeding to the shades of death." The words that follow, "Cujus animam gementem, contristantem, pertransivit gladius," have been thus embellished: "By the Mediator's Cross stood distressfully Mary and John, His Mother and His friend. Through the Mother's sad soul, yea through her very soul, pierced the sword." And in this whining and mincing strain runs the whole passage. The "Amen" alone is faithfully rendered by another Amen. It may, certainly, be said that if we except the first magnificent "grave," the translation, for the most part, accords with the music. But upon this point I must pronounce upon both the one and the other what Chateaubriand has said upon the latter in very eloquent language (*Genius of Christianity*, vol. ii. pp. 5-6): "Pergolesi has unfolded in the Stabat Mater all the resources of his art; but has he outdone the Plain-song of the Church? He has varied the music at each stanza, notwithstanding that the essential character of

On Misadaptations of Text.

Pergolesi's setting of which is also open to exception;

On Mis-adaptations of Text.

departing, as Chateaubriand points out, from the monotony proper to grief.

sorrow lies in the repetition of the same sentiment, and, so to speak, in the monotony of grief. Tears may flow from various causes, but they have always a common bitterness; besides, it is seldom that people weep for a multitude of ills in the aggregate, and, when wounds are numerous, there is always one more poignant than the rest, which eventually engrosses the lesser pains. Such is the secret of the charm of our old French romances. The same melody, recurring at each couplet to different words, is a perfect counterpart of nature. A person who is distressed in mind allows his thoughts to range over a variety of subjects, while the foundation for his sorrows is always one and the same. Now Pergolesi has failed to recognise this truth, which flows from the theory of the passions; for, according to his treatment, no one mental sigh resembles the one that preceded it. Wherever there is variety, there will always be found to be distraction; and wherever there is distraction, sadness is at an end."

Grievous, indeed, is it to find so renowned a sacred poet as Klopstock holding up to others so bad an example; but yet more grievous that many living composers should connive at the same thing—among them even Beethoven, who, with his great and original gifts, should have been the last to admit anything of inferior quality. Yet how constrained, how theatrical, how often utterly vapid is the text upon which his oratorio of "Christ at the Mount of Olives" is founded! But I pass this over, because, according to modern fashion, it has become an almost invariable rule that the material of oratorios and operas should be drawn from a common stock; a practice whereof the work in question affords, I fear, abundant evidence. But what is it that Beethoven has been content to do in his purely ecclesiastical compositions, or, at least, what is it that others have unworthily put upon him? A reference to his Mass in C for four voices (Op. 86) will show. The opening words are quite simple,

On Misadaptations of Text.

Text of Beethoven's "Mount of Olives;"

of the Mass in C.

On Misadaptations of Text.

but lofty in character, when sung with unaffected fervour, and because they are so sung, the singer dwells with satisfaction upon a single idea. In place of the old "Kyrie eleison, Christe eleison," we now find in this Mass the following prosaic piece of poetry, in which, too, Christ is altogether forgotten: "Low in the dust we adore Thee, Eternal Ruler of the world, the Almighty One. Who can name Thee, who comprehend Thee? Thou Infinite! Yea, immeasurable, unspeakable in Thy might! Like children lisp we the Name of God." The wonderful "Gloria in excelsis Deo" which follows, is, again, interlarded with honey in exactly the same way: "Praise, love, and thanks be to Thee;" and the simple "Et in terra pax hominibus bonæ voluntatis," is represented by "In silent awe we behold thy wonders, for by Thee and through Thee, we exist, live, and breathe." And so it goes on; so that we may picture the great composer to ourselves as like Demosthenes, who studied the art of speaking beside a roaring waterfall, with his mouth full of stones. Better a text of pure prose, unhampered by rhyme or rhythm, yet plain and weighty—if indeed there is to be a translation at all — than this bombastic, flowery language, altogether unsuited to the church.

On Misadaptations of Text.

The worst trick is that played with Mozart's "Misericordias Domini," very methodically composed on a given plan. The text consists, if I may so say, of two short phrases, "Misericordias Domini" (the loving-kindness of the Lord), "cantabo in æternum" (will I sing for ever); but substantially of one only. For either the "Misericordias Domini," or the "Cantabo in æternum," must be taken as the main idea. If the former, then the "Cantabo" must be subordinated to it; but if the latter, a singer whose soul is in the music must temper his jubilation with the thought of mercy. Could any one help laughing at a preacher who began softly with "the mercy of the Lord," and then immedi-

Character of Mozart's "Misericordias Domini" ruined by the German text.

On Misadaptations of Text.

ately continued exultingly, "I sing for ever"? Yet, for the sake of producing an artist's favourite contrast of colour—an object to which even Handel sacrificed much—Mozart has so contrived that the "Misericordias Domini" should be sung softly as a "grave," and the "Cantabo in æternum" loudly, to a brisk fugal subject. When this has been fully worked out, the "grave" recurs, and then once more the fugue. In the German edition, in common use, we find such pretty phrases given us to sing as in place of "Misericordias Domini," "My praise ever ascends to the Lord," and so on. In this way exultation is turned into supplication, and humility into exultation. Thousands of similar instances might be adduced, and, conversely, perhaps, just as many cases where good words are coupled to totally unsuitable music.

In making these remarks I am by no means asserting that, with the old church music, the diction invariably breathes the spirit of poetry, or that the great ancient composers for the church always paid due regard to prosody. I am quite as well aware that the earlier hymns contain many redundant words, as that the musicians of those times were not sufficiently attentive to metre. But I have a right to ask that the case should be fairly judged as a whole; and I would therefore ask, what sacred poems of our time there are which in depth, in spirit, and in fervour, approach the old hymns; or what modern musicians are there of real talent who have proved themselves masters of prosody? Moreover, this has to be considered. The text must, by its leading ideas, directly influence the setting; but a precise observance of the quantity of each particular syllable is not unfrequently impossible from the exigencies of the music: nay, carried beyond a certain point, it becomes positively pedantic, as it would be in mere speech. A schoolmaster, who made his boys scan, might make them read the Lord's Prayer in so

On Misadaptations of Text.

Faults of prosody in the old church music.

On Mis-adaptations of Text.

Accent not to be too much insisted on.

strictly correct a manner as to bring the long and short syllables into sharp contrast. But an impassioned preacher will be compelled in the glow of his declamation to soften down much of this; just as in the recital of a poem we should expect, as a matter of taste, the framework of the versification not to be brought too prominently into view. The strictures, therefore, passed upon the old composers entirely disappear when we regard their truly inspired, sustained, and measured music, and when they are rendered with that refinement of feeling that the words go hand in hand with the music, yet not so as if it were the sole object doggedly to impress upon the notes the quantity of each long and short syllable. The true theory of music should aim, therefore, at laying down with judgment such rules as shall reconcile dry prosody with instinctive feeling. Such rules, however, have, I fear, not been hitherto evolved in our day; though, perhaps, when a composition is by way of being framed according to rule, we sometimes have regularly constructed pieces with notes accurately dotted and tailed, which no more breathe a poetical spirit than if a whole school were to pronounce their syllables to a prescribed musical beat. Perhaps, however, in this last I am saying too much; and I shall content myself with asking this question for my own information: which of our modern theorists has written exhaustively on the question— whether the prosody of each word is to be allowed absolutely to govern the music; and are our compositions to be such that a punctilious teacher of grammar could prescribe their periods?

On Misadaptations of Text.

ON CHORAL SOCIETIES.

On Choral Societies.

Public concerts unsatisfactory.

OUR public performances of music are subject to so many paramount influences, that no mere individual can effect anything towards the removal of their numerous defects. Nothing short of positive exhaustion will some day bring it about, that, disgusted with the rubbish they ought from the first to have rejected, people will, for the sake of change, once more have recourse to forgotten treasures.

Value of private societies.

The materials at the command of individuals are generally insufficient for the formation of more than a private musical society; and it is devoutly to be wished that such societies were established universally. They will bring their own reward with them. For

PURITY IN MUSICAL ART.

On Choral Societies.

a faithful miniature copy has almost the same value as the full-size picture; and the executive skill and sympathetic feeling of a small body may, perhaps, make up for the absence of performances on a large scale. There is, too, fine vocal part-music, which is best heard when rendered by skilled vocalists in single parts. Latrobe, in the preface to the third volume of his Selection of Sacred Music (London, 1806), speaks with rapture of a musical family in England, and adds, " I have heard the best vocal pieces of Handel and other great masters rendered with greater precision and true feeling in this family circle than one usually hears from professionals at public performances."

Private societies may have for their objects either instrumental or vocal music. Delightful in the highest degree it is when there are both kinds; at the same time it will not be easy to combine them satisfactorily in a simultaneous performance: and it can well be afforded that they should be independent

Better, as a rule, exclusively vocal or exclusively instrumental.

of each other; for there are a multitude of the most beautiful pieces for instruments only, and a still larger number of first-rate works adapted for vocal rendering only. Vocal works which confessedly cannot be got up at all without instrumental accompaniment, like Haydn's Creation, may be left to such localities as rejoice in an abundance of musical talent of all kinds. But this will still leave a large store as the peculiar possession of good private societies,—music which must be regarded as almost extinct; viz., genuine old Chorales, old music of the pure church style, and national songs, besides the greater part of compositions, chiefly Italian, of the oratorio class.

If the object be to raise and edify the mind by music, choral societies are certainly entitled to rank as the foremost means to that end. For if composers have been inspired by beautiful words, their inspiration must have impressed itself distinctly upon the music they wrote; and what is there that can be

On Choral Societies.

Vocal societies superior in moral influence.

compared to the human voice when lofty ideas sway the singer's soul?

For a number of years I have taken an active part in a choral society, which may pride itself on having, with the utmost zeal, and upon an extensive historical plan, made a high standard its aim and object. Thus, observing what went on immediately around me, and taking note of the proceedings of others, I have had much opportunity for reflection upon choral societies; whence it may not improbably be of general service, if I take leave to offer the following remarks upon them, particularly as attention can be more readily compelled by print than by word of mouth. In doing this, I do not pretend to dictate to masters of the art. It would be worse than presumption if I were to read a lecture to men like Zelter upon their duties in any respect whatsoever. But inasmuch as the best men,—those who have acquainted themselves with the history of the subject,—are just the most reticent,

On Choral Societies.

Personal experience on the subject.

On Choral Societies.

it may perhaps be permitted to an amateur, who has reflected upon it, to put in a word, and at all events to try to give a helping hand to a good cause.

Essential difference between two types of choral societies.

If we take choral societies as a whole, it is impossible to lay down absolutely what is the best way of conducting them. Thus, if the object be light entertainment, they are as laudable as any social gathering can be; but then, of course, the way in which they are conducted will differ altogether from what it would be if the society met together for the enjoyment of classical music, with a view to the edification and refinement of the mind, and its diversion from the ordinary affairs of life. It is only of this latter class that I shall here speak, for it is through them alone that some sort of relief can be given to the pressing musical wants of the day; so far, that is, as such societies are steadily bent on becoming familiar with the purest and most finished specimens of every type, and admit works of indifferent merit, not from choice, but simply as a makeshift from time to time, conducing to a better knowledge of what is highest and best.

" The first and most essential condition for such a society is that the members are judiciously chosen, that genuine lovers of art combine together, that care is taken to secure an equal distribution of voices, and to nourish to the full the love and enjoyment of true art. Consequently, an evening devoted to singing must take precedence of all ordinary eating and drinking engagements; and all the members must feel that an association that requires their united efforts to form and maintain must not be at the mercy of other ordinary pleasures, especially as, while in other gatherings the absence of one is not much felt, here the absence of a single voice may quite possibly bring the whole thing to a deadlock, and this even in choruses, where a single efficient voice may be an indispensable support to the rest. The conductor of the choral society must, therefore, exert himself to

On Choral Societies.

Necessary conditions of a good society.

Regular attendance.

On Choral Societies.

Earnestness

and good music.

the utmost to prevent the intrusion, to the detriment of its interests, of the frivolity and idleness permitted and permissible in relation to other amusements. If this line of action be steadily pursued from the first, and if the members of the society can count with certainty upon having classical compositions of all kinds put into their hands, the love of the thing will very quickly engender the needful interest without further prescription. If the society consist of members who may be credited with a high moral aim, they will soon see that there is a brighter sun in a cultivated and enthusiastic choir than in all the brilliant circles of fashion; nor will there then be any occasion for finding fault with any who profess themselves unable to devote themselves, heart and soul, for three hours in a week out of the hundred and sixty-eight, to so divine an art. When the society consists promiscuously of good and bad members, some indulgence is necessary, because the just distribution of the voices becomes

PURITY IN MUSICAL ART.

impracticable, and the better members must endure the vexation of having to put up with what is called the general effect, *i.e.* such bawling as penetrates through doors and windows.

A second prime requisite for a good choral society is a large musical library. For the very finest music is apt to pall from a continued absence of variety; whence it not unfrequently happens that the oftener the most beautiful pieces are gone through, the worse they are sung. So, again, instrumentalists find that the piece they have practised is often best played when resumed after being laid aside for a while. A scanty library is likely enough to cause people to contract bad likings for want of better material, and swallow grain and husk with equal relish. A point should therefore be made of representing side by side, in their finest works, a variety of masters, from the remotest to the present time. No one style, no one composer, nor the composers of any

On Choral Societies.

Necessity of a large library for sake of variety.

On Choral Societies.

one country, should be allowed an absolute predominance, nor should a whole evening on any account be devoted to the grave and measured music of the old church style, which, unaided by the imposing effect of a church, is apt to exhaust and overstrain the attention, while, even in a church, it is difficult to endure a long uninterrupted musical performance. Above all else, care should be taken to have not only four-part pieces, but pieces in one, two, or three parts, for all the different voices, and especially pieces in eight parts or more, the peculiar beauty of which last lies in their rising to a climax, not by dint of increased vocal effort, but by the accession of parts. It may often happen that there are only a few voices of the highest excellence, and this renders it very important to have the resource of an ample library, in order to make the fullest use of individual talent.

The acquisition of a good library has, however, many difficulties—difficulties which are, of course, insurmountable if the members of the society share the disposition of those many persons who can spend any amount on finery, trinkets, balls, and dinners, but decline acquaintance with good music unless offered gratuitously. No good can be done where such a paltry spirit prevails; but, if due liberality be forthcoming, good results may be hoped for. The best works of our countrymen, Handel, and Sebastian Bach, are, in great part, in print—Handel's almost without an exception in England, and partially in German editions, which, though a good deal mutilated, always contain much admirable matter. The original Hussite, Lutheran, and Calvinistic chorales may easily be got together. A choral society might even be content with the specimens appended to Mortimer's "Choral Music of the Period of the Reformation," Berlin, 1821, 4 vols. I have already indicated the national songs that may be had in print. The compositions of the old Flemish and Dutch school are

On Choral Societies.

Certain works recommended.

On Choral Societies.

indeed very hard to meet with. For Italian music, one is forced, as a rule, to search everywhere for manuscripts, not only in Rome (where, certainly, much may be obtained from Signor Fortunato Santini), but also in other places, because in Italy, as in Spain, a bad habit has always prevailed of each locality keeping its own productions to itself, or rating them as superior to anything else. There exist, however, in print, several considerable Italian works, either sacred or otherwise interesting to choral bodies: in particular, I may mention L. Leo's "Miserere" for eight voices, Pergolesi's "Stabat Mater," which is entirely ruined in Hiller's German edition, a Litany and Mass by Durante, for four voices, and the Collection mentioned at page 49, comprising Allegri's and Bai's "Misereres," and Palestrina's "Lamentationes," "Responsoria," "Popule meus," "Stabat Mater," and "Fratres ego enim." To these I should add some duets, and a Magnificat of Durante, lately published at Leipsig and Berlin, as well as Marcello's magnificent edition of the Psalms, recently prepared in Florence under Cherubini's directions, in 12 folio volumes. I do not mention other smaller pieces printed in periodicals, miscellaneous collections, or elsewhere; moreover, I may have overlooked a good many that have been printed, because I have always made it my chief object to procure from Italy itself the most authentic available MSS.

On Choral Societies.

A further duty attaching to the conductor of a society devoted to classical music is to look carefully after the practising of the separate parts. Thus, previous to the execution of the piece, all the sopranos should be practised together, so far as they need assistance, then the altos, and the rest—each part separately—and that too under the conductor's own direction, so that when he comes to direct the final performance, he may have no cause to be dissatisfied with the work of others. In this way only can the requisite steadiness and refinement

Method of conducting practices.

be secured. Numberless points, too, can can thus be noticed, which in simultaneous singing would remain unsettled, one part easily drowning another, and politeness and delicacy preventing corrections being made as freely as in more private intercourse. For accomplished vocalists, indeed, such preparations may be unnecessary, but in most cases they are indispensable. As a rule, too, it will be found that those who have a real taste for art are far from averse to practices, so long as compositions of first-rate quality in their different kinds are tendered to them; for the greater the effort involved in the pursuit of Beauty, the greater the appreciation of it. Accomplished vocalists have also the satisfaction of administering by their own example salutary encouragement and instruction to those who are not so proficient. And how easy is it to spare a couple of by-hours, provided a man knows how in other respects to economise his time!

Thus far, I have made no reference to

public performances, to which many persons are very partial, either from vanity, or because from good-nature they would have all the world share in their pleasure. If choral societies aim at comprehensive historical knowledge, and devote their best energies to those masterpieces that take us aside from worldly ways, a constant appearance in public on their part would be as paradoxical a proceeding as to invite educated and uneducated alike, without distinction of persons, to listen to the recital of a profoundly conceived poem. That certain pieces may be brought to a public hearing, and under certain circumstances must be so brought, as showing a wish to give pleasure, is natural enough. But I have become more convinced every year that privacy, except for a few intimate friends, is of the greatest consequence to choral societies; for thus, and thus only, can be engendered that calm and even temper essential to a serious passion for music. It secures you, moreover, from laboured effort; for in a

On Choral Societies. Frequent performances in public better avoided, if the society has a high musical aim.

On Choral Societies.

public performance the smallest errors must be avoided, and their complete avoidance usually requires over much pains from unpretending amateurs. It is always better quietly to pass over slight defects, but to atone for them by abundant excellence. Similarly, in literature it is far better to have a general acquaintance with classic authors, and to risk the misapprehension of a word here and there, than to exhaust the whole of one's energies over one favourite volume.

Obstacles, such as prejudice and bad training, requiring patience to surmount.

But while the society closes its doors to the outside world, in order to essay at leisure the execution of first-rate musical works with a select few, it will always be necessary for the conductor of a well-constituted society to exercise an unwearied patience and a kindly indulgence; for, from the education, or, I should say, mis-education of our people, their minds are usually, not as a fresh and virgin soil, but preoccupied with certain notions, which prevent the highest form of art from being appreciated at first, though afterwards it reveals its overpowering charm, as I well know from experience. It must be remembered, too, that classical music must always have its particular foes, whose censure is in reality its highest praise, as well as that we have in this lower world of ours a pretty large number who can see quickly enough a great deal in what is gay and lively, but are unable without much effort to grasp the profound intention and angelic purity of a different style. This indeed is more to be expected now than ever, as a youthful taste for music of this latter kind is hardly cherished by one of our churches, whereas it is of infinite importance that the appreciation of the highest art should be inculcated in the time of youth. We have only to read Zelter's most interesting memoir of his friend Fasch (Berlin, 1801) to realise the difficulties with which high art has to contend. To the want of preparatory training and faculty of apprehension must be added the dearth of

On Choral Societies

On Choral Societies.

strong deep altos and basses, which are much needed for a good many of the older masterpieces, those especially of Josquin, Senffel, Lasso, and Palestrina. For such works as these I have to be content, as best may be, with a woodcut instead of a picture, and to draw upon my imagination to supply the deficiency. But many will not be disposed to tax their imagination for such kindly assistance, and so at times it may be necessary to leave several most admirable compositions unessayed.

The choice of a conductor all-important.

But in every case the cardinal point is the choice of a good conductor; one versed in classical music, able to grasp the score, and unyielding either to self-conceit or to the vanity of others. But this, alas! is precisely the point, where with musical societies of every kind, least care is taken. Only too often there are found installed in arbitrary authority either amateurs, who know little or nothing of their duty, and like the cook in Lichtenberg's Short Essays, can at best assert themselves to be endowed with capital appetites, or else assuming professionals, in whose eyes their own laboured handiwork and their own compositions are superior to anything else. Either way the case is deplorable, but the latter decidedly more so than the former. I mean that ignorance is at all events usually disposed to profit with a good grace by the superiority of others, whilst a musical autocrat of the ordinary stamp is the most intolerable creature on earth. He has so high an opinion of himself, and is so constantly occupied with composing, that he never gives his attention to classical music, and his self-esteem generally causes him to fall foul of all around him, so that he himself may become conspicuous on the ground he has levelled. Our unceasingly prolific composers often remind me of a learned old friend who was always writing himself, but never read the writings of others. When a pointed allusion to it was made to his wife, the good woman haughtily replied, " My husband has

On Choral Societies.

no need to buy books, for he writes his own books." This applies to thousands at the present day, who plume themselves on their own writings, and would suppress all classical music. For the same reason certain concerts, given much too frequently, can only be described as pitiful exhibitions, where bald and soulless excercitations are to be heard. It would be well to say to the conductors of most of our choral societies, as well as to most of our young poets, "Do as you please, but spare us your own compositions." No doubt a healthy germ may sometimes be crushed by so stringent a rule; but it will be consoling to know that the conductor is thus left free to select the choicest works of acknowledged classical authors for practice. So it is that nature allows many a small bird to perish that eagles may be nourished. At the same time there may well be exceptions, where the conductor may really rank as a great composer. It would be found a good safeguard, the society being provided in the first in-

Caution as to conductors' own compositions.

stance with the best standard works, and having practised them diligently, not to allow a conductor who is so much given to composing to put forward his own productions, unless requested to do so; but take care that he does not show beforehand that he would wish to be so requested, and that he does not set himself up for a great composer. If the society does not possess a good library, want of material may indeed throw you back upon your conductor's own resources, or upon the perpetual repetition of the same pieces. But the proverb, "Necessity is above law," can never prove, except for the truth it conveys, an agreeable lesson.

On Choral Societies.

Then, I unhesitatingly recommend the entire exclusion of operas, at any rate of the modern popular operas, much talent though there be in portions of them. The range of classical works outside of opera is of boundless extent, and demands an even balance of mind, especially nowadays when the music that one hears from one's earliest days

Opera should be excluded.

On Choral Societies.

onwards has a wanton and worldly influence, which causes everything lying outside opera to wear a strange sort of look from want of familiarity with it; and this strangeness can only be dispelled by reserving certain hours, in which the whole attention may be concentrated on other styles than the operatic. Moreover, one really hears the modern opera music wherever one goes. Germany is now overrun with theatres; the music brought out in them is sedulously reproduced at concerts; and social gatherings are always seeking their musical cheer in opera music. The whole time, too, that remains out of the one hundred and sixty-eight hours of the week, after deducting therefrom the short harmonic evening, may be devoted, if need be, to a diligent cultivation of opera at home. Any one, then, who, in view of all this worldly enjoyment, would still demand that a choral society should undertake modern opera, and thereby expose itself to an imputation of frivolity, is like the smoker who, at the confessional, took his lighted pipe out of his mouth, and, holding it behind his back, began his confession with the request to be allowed to continue smoking meanwhile.

On Choral Societies.

Several other points, too often regarded as of secondary moment, deserve the most careful attention. Foremost among them I reckon this—that the conductor of the society should make the expression clearly and accurately understood, to which end he should, with all possible care, go through those parts in which the expression is left, as is usually done in all the old scores, to the individual judgment. It is almost incredible how much a piece gains by the simultaneous observance of its fortes, pianos, crescendos, and diminuendos. If these are not clearly indicated in the copies of the parts, two evils must necessarily arise, the one as bad as the other—either the singing will be without feeling, and so spiritless throughout, or else each singer will be guided by his own feeling, and the requisite unity of effect be entirely lost.

Marks of expression to be inserted in score of old music.

On Choral Societies.

Full indications of expression have indeed their great difficulties, and, in attempting them it will not be found easy exactly to reconcile different tastes; yet a fixed rule is always preferable to untutored liberty, which either remains inactive from timidity, or else throws the whole choir into confusion.

Translations sometimes necessary.

Next, it is extremely important for the society to engage a skilful translator. For while it is in my judgment quite necessary, on account of the beauty of the words, to have the Latin and Italian text sung in the original, the meaning of the words must always be made perfectly clear to the singers. But as regards other languages this practice cannot hold good, and there German words must be substituted for singing in lieu of the original text, because otherwise it is impossible to reckon upon its being even correctly pronounced. Such substitution is often, must be confessed, a very troublesome task but who that cares for the object in view will shrink from the labour?

Lastly, I would point out a matter on which, small as it may appear, a great deal depends; and that is the desirability of indicating, by progressive numbers, the bars in the score of every piece, and in the separate vocal parts, and of continuing them, so far as may be, uninterruptedly throughout. This is the only means of specifying quickly and accurately the places where a stumble occurs, and to which, therefore, it will be necessary to revert. To be always counting with the finger is most troublesome, and may easily cause confusion, miscalculation on somebody's part being generally inevitable. Those who have taken part in sonatas for two players will at once see how greatly the labour of practising would be lightened if each bar were numbered. I should also advise that, in writing out the parts, the same cleff should invariably be used for each respective part. For example, the alto part should be always transcribed in the alto cleff, or always in the violin cleff; for few singers

On Choral Societies.

Bars to be numbered.

Cleffs to be uniform.

PURITY IN MUSICAL ART.

On Choral Societies.

of either sex are equally familiar with different clefs, and no advantage can accrue from choosing at one time one clef, at another time another, merely because scores may be marked with different clefs. Copyists easily acquire the requisite facility of transposing if they are properly looked after at first.

Attention to details well worth the trouble.

Many persons may not like my plea for a strict observance of rule in what may be called trifling matters, no less than in all others. I, on the other hand, have still less liking for a choral society being converted into a Babel. Without attention to details there can be no perfection, and regularity is, as Kant used to say, quite as easy, and even easier, to any one habituated to it, than irregularity.

Pleasures of classical music infinite, enduring, and divine.

Once more: if classical music has to encounter the prejudice of being considered as of too serious and exacting a nature, such prejudice can only proceed from levity or ignorance. On the part of well-conducted choral societies it can be, at all events, only senseless prejudice. For if such societies occupy themselves with the four descriptions of music commended in the foregoing pages— viz. genuine old chorales of various churches, compositions in the pure ecclesiastical style, compositions in the oratorio style, and, lastly, select national songs of all countries—they will then have at their command so abundant a store of the grave and gay, of the vehement and the tender, of the devotional and the racy, of the profound and the romantic, that it would be no exaggeration for any one to express the thought that has often come to me, and is no mere fancy, [that I could never grow old in spirit if a kind destiny were to preserve to me all my life long an unimpaired enjoyment of fine music.] Such has also been the feeling of the many accomplished amateurs who have been associated with me for a series of years. And I can assert that nothing has confirmed me in, and prompted me to, the contemplation of what is noble and

On Choral Societies.

On Choral Societies.

great, so much as the enthusiasm and the lively appreciation of which I have seen so many gratifying proofs throughout almost the whole of my intercourse with them. And thus to me, engaged as I am in the assiduous discharge of laborious professional duties, fine music, nourishing a bright flame in the soul, has become as precious as the noonday sun. Often have I repeated from my very soul with Luther, and will here repeat once more: "Music is a fair and glorious gift from God. I would not for the world renounce my humble share of Music."

www.ingramcontent.com/pod-product-compliance
Lightning Source LLC
Chambersburg PA
CBHW031816220426
43662CB00007B/679